**PILKINGTON'S ROYAL LANCASTRIAN POTTERY AND TILES**

PLATE 1. Lustre vase by Gordon Forsyth, dated 1908, height 20in.
Courtesy Manchester City Art Gallery.

# PILKINGTON'S ROYAL LANCASTRIAN POTTERY AND TILES
## BY
## A J CROSS

PREFACE
BY
BEVIS HILLIER

PUBLISHED
BY
RICHARD DENNIS
144 Kensington Church Street
London w8

First published 1980
All rights reserved.

©Anthony J Cross 1980
©Bevis Hillier 1980
©Richard Dennis 1980

Design by Gordon House
Origination by TPS, London
Printed in England by The Hillingdon Press, Uxbridge

ISBN 0 7153 6938 5

# CONTENTS

| | |
|---|---|
| page 6 | ACKNOWLEDGEMENTS |
| 7 | PREFACE |
| 10 | CHAPTER I HISTORY OF THE COMPANY |
| 17 | CHAPTER II TILES |
| 25 | CHAPTER III CRYSTALLINE AND OTHER GLAZES |
| 33 | CHAPTER IV THE SPREAD OF LUSTRE POTTERY AND ITS USE BY PILKINGTON'S |
| 43 | CHAPTER V POTTERY |
| 53 | CHAPTER VI DESIGNERS AND ARTISTS |
| 75 | CHAPTER VII IDENTIFICATION MARKS |
| 82-90 | APPENDICES I-V |
| 91 | SELECTED BIBLIOGRAPHY |
| 92 | INDEX |

# ACKNOWLEDGEMENTS

I wish to acknowledge all those who have assisted in the formation of this work; Richard Dennis, who suggested the idea, the many people who have contributed reference material, pottery and tiles for the illustrations, in particular the Marquis of Dufferin and Ava, Geoffrey Godden, Brian Ball, A. and Miss M. Chambers, M. W. Devereaux, T. B. Jones, John Rabbets, and Mary McLoughlin. Also to Mr. D. Bleazard and Prudence Cuming who took the photographs, Gordon House whose design work has been *sans reproche*, and the curators of the museums, art galleries and libraries of Manchester, Blackburn, Bolton, Salford, Eccles, Bury, Warrington, Swinton and Pendlebury, Stoke, and the Victoria and Albert Museum.

I am especially indebted to the directors of Pilkington's Tiles Ltd particularly Lawrence Burton for their assistance in making company records and archival material available for study and for permission to quote from their catalogues and other publications, which are presented in the appendix. I also acknowledge the assistance provided by members of the Burton and Pilkington families and members of staff, both past and present, of Pilkington's Tiles Ltd.

The plates in this volume are reproduced by courtesy of the following: B. H. Tetlow Ltd; Blackburn Museum and Art Gallery; Bolton Museum and Art Gallery; Manchester City Art Galleries; Manchester Polytechnic; Nordenfjeldske Kunstindustrimuseum, Trondheim; North Staffordshire Library, Hanley; Pilkington's Tiles Ltd; Raymond Ades Collection; Salford Art Gallery and Museum; Staatliche Antikensammlungen und Glyptothec, Munich; Swinton Central Library; Victoria and Albert Museum; Walker Art Gallery.

Finally, I should like to thank Mr. T. A. Lockett, whose assistance in the preparation of the manuscript has been invaluable.

A. J. Cross 1980

# PREFACE

The first book written on Pilkington's Royal Lancastrian Pottery was published in 1957 by Abraham Lomax, who was chemist at the works from 1896 to 1911. In the years which have elapsed since Lomax's book appeared, Lancastrian Pottery has become far better known and appreciated by collectors–although it is still not a name which springs to mind when Art Nouveau pottery or late-Victorian lustreware are mentioned, in the way that William De Morgan's name does. It is right that Lomax's highly personal account–the moving tribute of an 'old factory hand' to his brother craftsmen–should now be supplemented by a cooler, more objective appraisal; and that is what Mr Cross has achieved in this admirable book.

The factory which came into being in 1891 at Clifton, about five miles north of Manchester, through an accidental discovery of clay in the course of faulty coal-mining engineering, was no amateurish local enterprise, but an up-to-the-minute undertaking which epitomised its historical period in several ways. In the first place, it secured as manager an outstanding scientist–William Burton, a young chemist from Wedgwood's–who was himself the very type of the new kind of self-made man. A grocer's son, he had taken advantage of the new opportunities of public education, had studied chemistry at the Royal School of Mines, South Kensington, and had thoroughly familiarised himself with the pottery business. (In the same way, the potter George Tinworth climbed up from a similar background, also training at South Kensington, though in the art rather than the science of potting.) This was an age of great technical advances; potters could no longer afford to ignore the prescriptions of science. It was a time of heady experiment; Mr Cross records that the War Office even asked Pilkington's to research into the possibility of pottery bullets.

Secondly, the Lancastrian pottery was committed to the new Art Nouveau style. One wonders whether any other Victorian factories could boast such a distinguished company of pioneer Art Nouveau designers as Walter Crane (claimed by modern writers on Art Nouveau, such as Robert Schmutzler, as the first leading practitioner of the style), Frederick Shields, C.F.A. Voysey and Lewis Day, who wrote so many 'how-to-do-it' books for students of drawing and design. Pilkington's even had the prince of Art Nouveau designers on their payroll: at the 1901 Glasgow Exhibition they showed four panels with designs by Alphonse Mucha, the great posterist.

Art Nouveau gave to the factory's wares their characteristic shapes; but one notices in the wares the typical 1890s obsession with colour. In 1888 M.G. Puchet published in the *Revue Scientifique* a short study of the colour-sense in literature; approaching his subject as a physiologist's holiday-task, he noted the number of times colour-words occurred in each of five French authors' works. In *España Moderna* of March 1894 Dr Thebussen published a paper on 'Lo Verde', in which he proved that Cervantes had a special predilection for green. And to *The Contemporary Review* of May 1896 (when the Lancastrian Pottery was in its first flourishing period), Havelock Ellis contributed a long paper on 'The Colour Sense in Literature', analysing more extensively than Puchet the incidence of different colours in the works of classic authors, and coming to certain psychological conclusions about the use of colours: red is the colour of blood and love, black, white and yellow (colours 'that are rare in the world') are the colours of 'golden impossibilities' and so on. In France, Seurat and Monet were experimenting with the spectrum palette. Lomax, in his 1957 book, showed how the new interest in colour effects was manifested in ceramics:

> 'Tiger Eye' crystalline glazes were produced at Rookwood, USA. Theodore Deck in France produced pottery in the style of the Ancient Persians, so did William De Morgan here. At the Paris exhibition of 1900, glazes bearing radiating crystals on their surface were shown. Bernard Moore in Staffordshire was producing his *Rouge Flambé* wares, and coloured glazed wares were being made by Howson Taylor at Birmingham. After the turn of the century, Messrs. Doulton put their well-known Flambé glazed pottery on the market in 1910, and in 1913, Mr. Moorcroft began producing his fine 'Powder Blue' glazed ware. In the midst of this ferment Lancastrian Pottery made its startling appearance.

We may note, in passing, the 'decentralisation' of the pottery industry, away from the traditional nucleus of Staffordshire: of the potters specialising in colour-effect wares, De Morgan was in Chelsea, Merton

Abbey, and Fulham; Doulton's were at Lambeth; Howson Taylor's Ruskin Pottery was at Birmingham; and Pilkington's were near Manchester.

The taste for plain colour (at the Lancastrian pottery, 'Kingfisher Blue', 'Orange Vermilion' and 'Uranium Orange' were favourites) and for abstract colour effects, was in tune with the general reaction of Art Nouveau away from 'historicism' (ie, decoration which either portrayed historical or anecdotal episodes, or which was based on an historical style, for example, Renaissance 'lambrequins'). Abstract art occurred in pottery before it appeared in painting; when Gordon Forsyth, Pilkington's superb designer, saw the bent and twisted steelwork of the gutted British section of the Brussels Exhibition, destroyed by fire in 1910, he developed the theme, painting (according to Lomax) 'a large vase with leaping, surging, swirling tongues of lurid flame' in lustre glaze.

With great skill and detail, Mr Cross sets the Royal Lancastrian Pottery in its historical and artistic context; the book will also be of immense use to the rapidly growing body of collectors of these glowing wares.

BH

PLATE 1. Moulded tile signed Kwiatkoski, circa 1900, 12×8in. Courtesy Bolton Museum and Art Gallery.

PLATE II. Crane's Figures Striped and Ogee by Richard Joyce, dated 1910, height 10in.

PLATE III. An early trial lustre for Crane's Lion Bowl design, unsigned, circa 1905, height 6½in, and the bowl painted by William S. Mycock, dated 1932, height 5in.

PLATE IV. Designed by Walter Crane, painted by Richard Joyce, dated circa 1919, height 12¼in.

PLATE V. Crane's Sea Maiden painted by (1) Richard Joyce, dated 1907, height 10½in. (2) Richard Joyce, dated 1906, height 10in. (3) William S. Mycock, dated 1916, height 10½in.

PLATE VI. Crane's Bon Accord painted by Richard Joyce, dated 1907, height 9in. Courtesy Manchester City Art Gallery.

PLATE VII. Crane's Night and Morning painted by Richard Joyce, dated 1906, diameter 12in.

# CHAPTER I
# HISTORY OF THE COMPANY

The first mention of Clifton appears in legal documents of the twelfth century, the main industry being agriculture. By the middle of the eighteenth century and after many changes of ownership the estate passed into the hands of the Fletcher family, one of the foremost coal-mining families in and around Bolton. Eventually coal-mining became an established industry and by the middle of the nineteenth century had begun to supersede the traditional agriculture and handloom weaving.

In 1865 Edward and Alfred Pilkington arrived to manage the local collieries on behalf of their uncles, Joseph and Josiah Evans, who had leased the collieries and mining rights from the Fletchers. Two years later, the Pilkingtons and their uncles took over the collieries completely and the Clifton and Kearsley Coal Company was formed. Two more of the Pilkington brothers, Laurence and Charles, joined the company and by 1885 the Pilkingtons were in sole control, Joseph Evans having died and Josiah retired.

About 1888 the coal seam at Botany Bay Pit was becoming exhausted and two new shafts were being sunk for what was intended to be Pepper Hill colliery, but unfortunately the drillers drove through the Great Red Rock Fault, also known as the Pendleton Fault, and the drilling had to be abandoned because of flooding. However, during the sinking of the two shafts, quantities of red marl had been discovered and it was thought that this could be used for the manufacture of building bricks. Through James Lee-Wood, the secretary of the coal company, consultations took place with William Burton, a chemist at Josiah Wedgwood & Sons, who suggested that the idea of brickmaking be abandoned in favour of tilemaking, there being at that time a demand for high-quality decorative tiles. This idea was accepted by the Pilkingtons, and in 1891 Pilkington's Tile and Pottery Company was formed with Laurence Pilkington as Chairman of the Board of Directors. As none of the Pilkingtons had experience of the pottery industry (their main function being to provide capital to invest in the new company), William Burton was invited to become manager, Burton was given the opportunity to design the layout of the plant, and together with his brother Joseph, who joined him about 1895, he guided the company through its formative years.

When William Burton first arrived at Clifton, to see the factory site, there were only open fields with no buildings whatsoever. It was possible therefore for the factory to be built along the then most modern lines. The works were planned by Burton himself without the aid of an architect and the layout is for the most part the same today. The building of the factory was no mean achievement for Burton; it was an enormous responsibility for a man under thirty years of age, yet he managed to overcome all the inherent problems associated with creating and running a new company in what was already a competitive industry.

Burton did have certain advantages, however. The site at Clifton was ideal, there was local labour, room to expand and, most essential, ready-made transport facilities—firstly Fletcher's canal which had been built to serve the collieries, and secondly the railway. The Manchester-Bolton line and the line serving north-east Lancashire joined a short distance from the works and gave the locality the name of Clifton Junction.

Although there was little specialised local labour, it was easily obtained from Burton's contacts in the potteries, and production began on 13 January 1893. Local labour was recruited nevertheless, and it was not uncommon for whole families to become employed at the factory and many employees served for over fifty years.

William Burton, in many senses the creator of the firm which bore the name of Pilkington, had not been brought up as a potter. He was born in 1863 in Manchester where his father had a small grocery business. His first work was as a pupil teacher, then as an elementary schoolmaster. After studying science at evening classes he became a science teacher in Manchester for the school board, but on obtaining a National Scholarship in Science he went to the Royal School of Mines, South Kensington, where he studied chemistry and the other branches of natural science.

In 1887 Burton went to Josiah Wedgwood & Sons to be their chemist, and he remained there for five years. During this time he acquired a good working knowledge of what was done in the potteries and gave two series of public lectures in Hanley, in connection with the Hanley Museum, on various periods in the history of pottery. In addition, he taught classes in technical pottery at the Wedgwood Institute, Burslem, and at the Mechanics Institute, Hanley. From 1897

Burton was an examiner in pottery manufacture for the City and Guilds of the London Examination Board and it was his opinion that the technical training of workmen, as such, should not be attempted in schools—but only in the workshop. When the Home Office proposed an impossible set of rules for the use and control of lead in the pottery industry, Burton took an active part in bringing the different sections of the trade together and played a leading part in formulating the regulations which were eventually adopted. For this service to the pottery industry he was presented with one large and two small richly embossed silver fruit stands, with two trays en suite. He also lectured extensively at art schools, at the English Ceramic Society and the Society of Arts—the latter presenting him with a silver medal for his paper 'Palette of the Potter' in 1896, an award later repeated for his paper 'Recent Advances in Pottery Decoration' given before them on 12 February 1901. In addition, he was the author of many books on ceramics. As a result of his chemical researches, many of which found practical uses, in 1908 Burton was awarded the honorary degree of Master of Arts by Manchester University.

As a manager, Burton took a great interest in the welfare and education of his staff, for example the workers in the lead house were given free milk to counter possible lead poisoning. Artists were encouraged in their work, some being taken to see the 1900 Paris Exhibition while student artists were sent to art schools to learn their trade, the company paying all their expenses. This latter practice is one which many companies carry out today and it is considered to be one of the more enlightened aspects of good management.

His efforts throughout this period were ceaseless and eventually the strain began to tell. In April 1915 his forthcoming retirement was announced and in July he finally retired. His employees presented him with an illuminated address in book form—the calligraphy being executed by Edward Johnston which they all signed, and with a silver bowl designed by J. B. Barraclough.

At the time of his retirement, Burton was recognised as one of the leading potters of the period, but in all his enterprises he had been greatly assisted by his brother, Joseph Burton. Joseph was born in 1868 and after his early schooling won an exhibition scholarship to the Royal College of Science in Dublin, where he studied chemistry, physics and minerology. His studies complete, he joined his brother William at Pilkington's where he was responsible for carrying out many experiments on glazes. Although working in the shadow of his more famous brother, he was nevertheless responsible for many of the successful researches into new glazes, and was a careful and thorough worker although not as extrovert a character

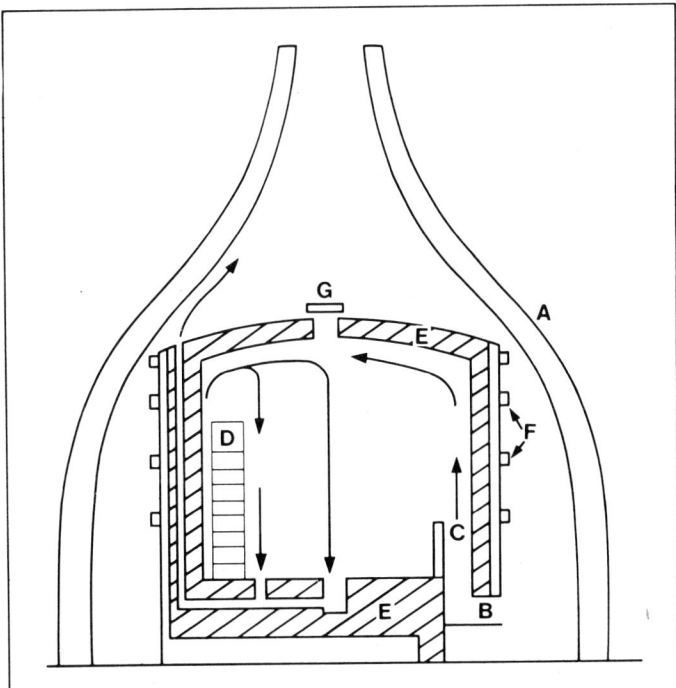

Fig. 1. Down-draught biscuit oven: A. bottle wall of common brick; B. firebox; C. bag-wall; D. saggars; E. firebrick; F. iron support bands; G. damper.

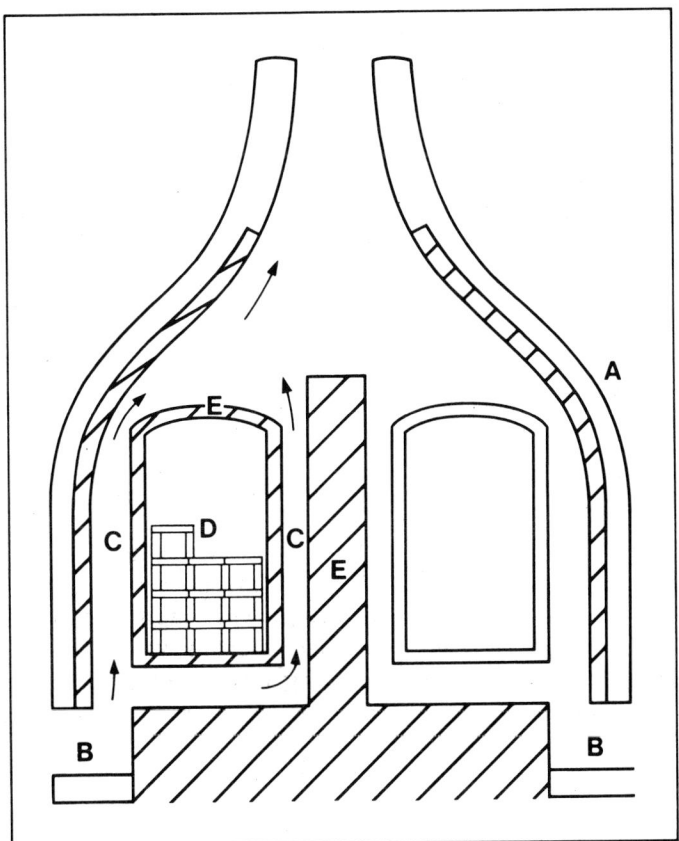

Fig. 2. Muffle glost kiln: A. bottle wall of common brick lined with firebrick; B. firebox; C. flue; D. kiln batts on pillars; E. firebrick.

as William. Both William and Joseph Burton were intensely interested in the products of the early potters, particularly the Chinese, Joseph being recognised as an authority on this subject. His knowledge of ceramic history was comprehensive and expert, and like his brother before him he frequently lectured on the techniques, art and history of pottery. On his death in 1934 his position as managing director was taken over by his son, David Burton. Unfortunately, unlike William and Joseph, David was not a potter, and he was unable to prevent a decline in sales of the pottery although tile production was increasing.

When the factory opened in 1893, two years after the company was formed, the emphasis was on tile manufacture, although from time to time small pottery items were made in order to demonstrate the new experimental glazes. From 1893 Pilkington's trade increased, so that by 1896 a new slip house, grinding plant, tile plant, bisque oven and placing shed were required to extend the company's business and by 1913 twenty-four kilns for tiles, seven biscuit ovens and three glost ovens were in operation.

Fig 1 shows a profile of a down-draught biscuit kiln, which was circular in shape with several fireboxes arranged around the circumference. The wares were placed in saggars ready for firing and the fires lit. As the firing got under way the control damper–open to begin with–was closed, so that the down-draught principle came into operation. The glazed ware was fired in a

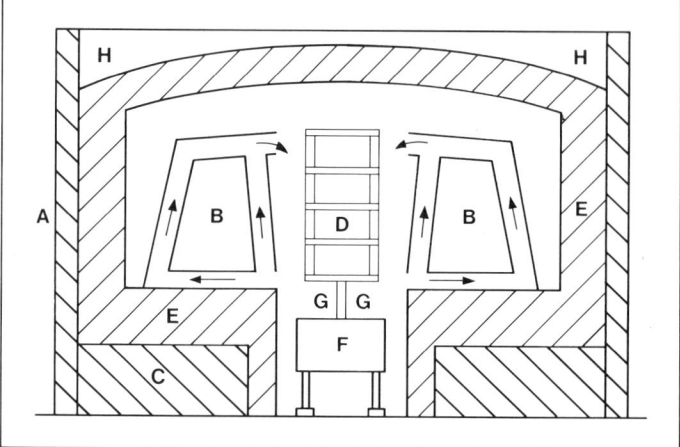

Fig. 3. Dressler tunnel kiln: A. common brick outer wall; B. combustion chamber; C. common brick; D. fireclay boxes; E. firebrick; F. truck; G. cubby holes; H. insulation.

muffle kiln (Fig 2). This comprised a pair of rectangular kilns with fireboxes down the outside walls. The items to be fired were placed in the kiln on batts supported by firebrick pillars, saggars being unnecessary since the products of combustion did not enter the kiln.

The company made reasonable profits from 1895 onwards but showed a loss of £124 in 1905, by which time pottery decorated by glaze effects only was being made and the production of lustre pottery was imminent. The company again made profits until 1917 when a loss of £13,516 was recorded. The following year this loss had been turned into a profit of £4,100,

PLATE 2. Pilkington's Tile and Pottery Co. Ltd., 1938. Courtesy Pilkington's Tiles Ltd.

PLATE VIII. Crane's Peacock painted by Charles Cundall, dated 1912, diameter 19in.

PLATE X. Crane's George and Dragon painted by Richard Joyce, dated 1910, diameter 19in. The title 'Un chevalier sans peur et sans reproche' was given to le Chevalier de Bayard an illustrious French knight who fought for François I.

PLATE XI. Selection of tiles from known designers, lower right by J.H. Rudd, next to this the design covering two tiles is attributed to C.F.A. Voysey. The remainder are all by Lewis F. Day.

PLATE IX. Tiles painted in Persian style, circa 1907.

PLATE XII. Selection of decorative tiles, circa 1895-1920.

which in 1919 was increased to £16,239. A record profit of £28,047 resulted in 1920 and from then onwards the company continued to prosper until World War II when production was reduced, and had it not been for Government contracts for the annealing of steel bars, carried out in the Dressler tunnel ovens, the firm would have been in serious financial difficulties. The situation was similar to that which had arisen during the Great War when tile production diminished and that of the lustre pottery was reduced to almost nothing. Government work had provided assistance in the form of contracts to produce ceramic filters for water purifiers, which had previously been imported from Germany, and Pilkington's had also been asked by the War Office to carry out experiments in the production of pottery bullets!

In 1921 a new step was taken when an agreement was signed with Dressler Tunnel Ovens Ltd to supply a new oven. This was to be 237ft in length with a capacity of 3,360yds of tiles per week. In the tunnel oven (Fig 3), the tiles were fired in shallow fireclay boxes stacked on a truck which ran on rails. At the entrance of the tunnel producer gas was fed into the combustion chambers, which ran on either side of the rails, mixed with air and ignited. The use of tunnel ovens had several advantages over the conventional kilns, the most important being that production was continuous making them considerably cheaper to run. The first Dressler oven began production in October 1921 and by 1938 five Dressler and two bisque tunnel ovens were in operation, replacing all but seven of the conventional bottle kilns. The latter were now used for pottery or for tile firing should any of the tunnels have broken down. Plate 2 shows the factory as it was in late 1938 and the various departments are shown in Fig 4.

The economic climate of the 1930s was such that the closure of the pottery section–in any case probably run for prestige purposes only–became inevitable towards the end of the decade, although a managing director in the mould of William Burton might have been able to prevent this. At a meeting of the directors in July 1936 the poor financial position of the pottery department

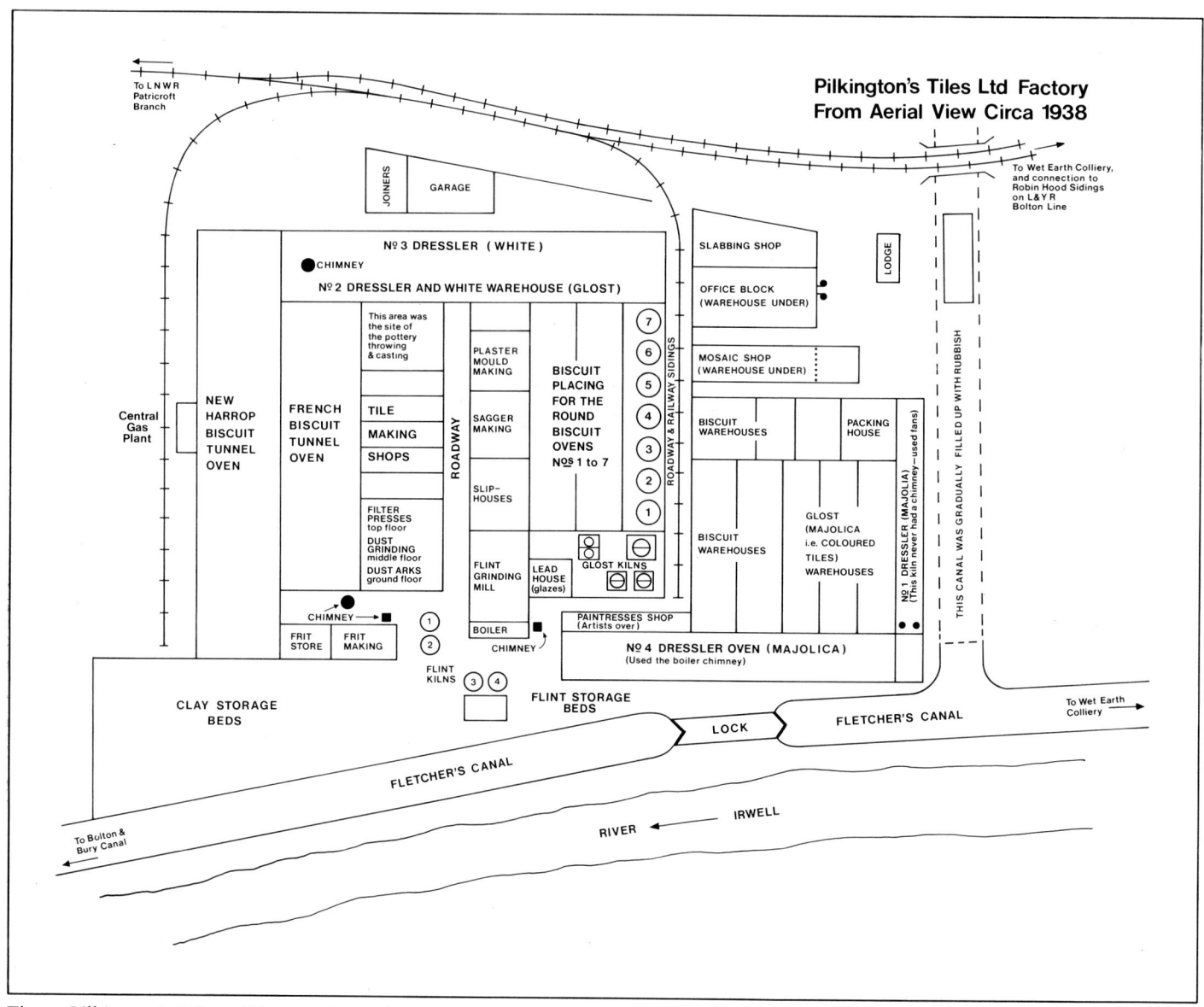

Fig. 4. Pilkington's Tile and Pottery Co. Ltd. 1938.

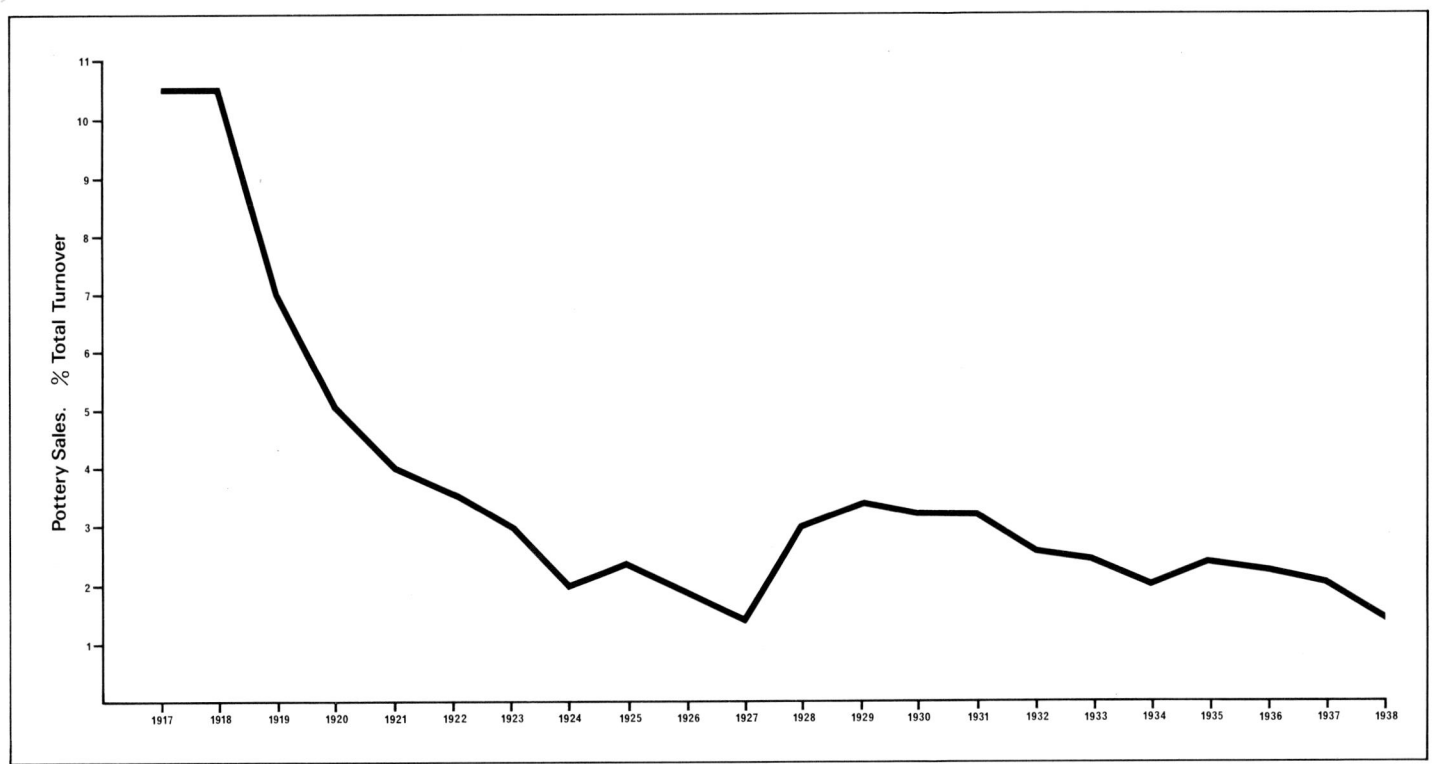

Fig. 5. Pottery sales as a percentage of total sales of tiles and pottery from 1917 to 1938. The introduction of lapis ware in 1929 appears as a peak in the falling sales.

was discussed, but the decision to close the pottery was deferred for twelve months. By August 1937, when the matter was raised again, the financial position had not improved, and so it was agreed that the pottery section should be closed down. The company's name was changed to Pilkington's Tiles Ltd. at an extraordinary general meeting of the directors in February 1938. The proportion of pottery to tile production had always been very small. The majority of pottery sold had been in the form of decorative glazed ware and, as will be seen in Chapter 4, very small numbers of lustre and other types of hand-painted pottery were produced. Figures before 1917 are not available, but the decline in turnover of the pottery compared to total sales from 10.5 per cent in 1917 to 1.3 per cent in 1938 is clearly illustrated in Fig 5, with a brief revival in the late twenties coinciding with the introduction of a new type of pottery known as lapis ware—of which more later.

The closure of the pottery department heralded the end of an era, but the desire of the company to manufacture quality pottery once more was revived briefly in the period 1948-57, but the ware bore little resemblance to its illustrious predecessor. Again the reason for closure was economic.

The tile business continued to expand, and in 1964 the company merged with Carter & Co of Poole, Dorset, in order to obtain additional production capacity. Carter's had been formed as a tile company in 1873 and had begun the production of pottery about 1880. The two companies therefore have similar histories of development and competed in the markets for decorative pottery, although Carter's products never really matched those of its Lancastrian rival, despite having in its employ such eminent artists as Harold and Phoebe Stabler and also John Adams. Decorative and functional pottery has been made by Carter's, or rather its subsidiary now known as Poole Pottery, for almost 100 years, and this experience was used to aid once more the production of Lancastrian Pottery—this time based at Blackpool. Manufacture of the new Lancastrian Pottery began in December 1972 and subsequently closed in December 1975, utilising some of the shapes which proved popular during the 1904-38 period. It remains to be seen if this ware proves to be as successful as its predecessors.

It is now ninety years since Pilkington's Tile and Pottery Company, managed by William Burton, began production. Under his guidance the company became established as a producer of high-quality tiles and pottery, exhibiting at international exhibitions where they were awarded many grands prix in competition with numerous other companies. Today the firm of Pilkington's Tiles Ltd. is one of the largest manufacturers of ceramic tiles in Britain, with about 60 per cent of the current tile production being decorated in some form, and it is a tribute to William and Joseph Burton that many of the glazes developed by them are still in use.

PLATE XIII. Tiles designed by Walter Crane and known as Flora's Train, 6×6in. Courtesy Victoria and Albert Museum.

PLATE XV. Panel of 6×6in. tiles designed by Gordon Forsyth. Courtesy Manchester City Art Gallery.

PLATE XIV. Part set of nursery rhyme tales in tubeline from designs by Margaret Pilkington, date circa 1920, size 9×6in.

PLATE XVI. Tile Panels showing pottery through the ages, designed by Gordon Forsyth. Courtesy Walker Art Gallery. Although undamaged when the building was bombed, it proved impracticable to rescue the panels and subsequently they were demolished.

# CHAPTER II
# TILES

Tiles were introduced into Britain by the Romans and were made in large quantities during the Roman occupation. With the decline of Roman influence, tile-making methods fell into disuse and tiles were not made again until after the Norman conquest. These were either glazed or unglazed and used in flooring (mainly for churches and abbeys). They were mostly of the encaustic type which were made by inlaying a pattern of coloured clay in a ground of another colour. The tiles were known as plastic-bodied, the clay being formed into the required shape and then fired. Modern tiles are made by compressing dried clay dust, a method first developed in Birmingham by Richard Prosser in 1833.

When production began at Pilkington's in 1893, a local clay body was used to manufacture tiles, but eventually the bulk of the materials was brought in from other parts of the country. The white earthenware tile body was made from an intimate mixture of china clay, ball clay, flint and china stone. The clays were brought from Cornwall, Devon and Dorset by ship and barge and unloaded at the company's own canal wharf. The clays were then stored in bulk on extensive weathering beds for several months and allowed to mature. Flint was imported from France or the south of England in the form of small boulders, calcined, and then crushed. The china stone obtained from Cornwall was simply crushed.

It was important for the calcined flint and china stone to be ground to the correct degree of fineness. To do this both materials were fed into large iron cylinders containing round flint pebbles and water. The cylinder then revolved, further crushing the calcined flint by the action of the pebbles against the hard interior of the cylinder. This process took about twenty-four hours to complete but checks were made periodically to ensure that the grinding was taking place correctly. The suspension of calcined flint and stone was run off and mixed with clay slip. The slip itself was produced by mulching the clay with water in iron vessels until the clay and water mixture had the consistency of cream. When the two suspensions had been thoroughly blended, the resulting mixture was sieved to ensure uniformity of the tile body.

This liquid tile mixture was then pumped into filter presses, where the superfluous water was extracted leaving behind cakes of plastic clay. In this state it could be used in the manufacture of plastic-bodied tiles, pottery or architectural faience. In order to convert the moist clay into dust, the plastic cakes were passed through drying chambers where the remaining moisture was removed. These dry cakes were dampened slightly and allowed to stand for some days, preparatory to grinding in a disintegrator. The damp dust from this machine, containing about 10 per cent water and as coarse as fine oatmeal, was then stored until needed.

Tiles were produced by feeding the dust into a steel die box and compressing it by a steel die. About 36,000 pressings could be carried out before the die had to be renewed. The tile so made then had its rough edges removed and was dried and fired. As has already been mentioned, bottle kilns were used for many years until replaced by tunnel ovens. During the biscuit firing, at about 1150°C, tiles contracted at the rate of a half inch to the foot. Following this firing, the tiles were grouped into their different sizes, for although tiles of the same size could be fired, the finished dimensions would vary depending on the temperature variations within the kiln and the place occupied by the tile.

From the biscuit firing, tiles were taken for glazing with plain enamels or for decorating by the painters and paintresses, whose duty it was to colour the designs already impressed or marked on to the tile. Coloured printed patterns were also used as a method of decoration, and tiles of this printed or embossed type, such as those illustrated in Plate 14, were used by range makers and furniture makers for incorporating into fireplaces, dressing-tables and wash-handstands. The styles of these designs were for the most part conventionally floral, but sometimes there was a tendency towards an Art Nouveau style. In 1898 Pilkington's won awards at the Winnipeg Industrial Exhibition for their majolica, decorative, hand-painted and printed tiles.

For many years tiles decorated in the simulated Persian fashion were produced, and tiles of this type were used for interior decoration on board the ill-fated Titanic. Tiles decorated in Persian style with blues and greens predominating, often spotted with globules of Rhodian red, were made from a plastic body, and examples of these are illustrated in Plate IX, 12.

Decorative tiles were produced by several techniques; either painted or printed underglaze often

PLATE 3. William Burton seated right, with his father and brothers. Joseph Burton is standing back row, left.

using several colour combinations, or a stencilled design in underglaze blue on white; tiles were painted in coloured glazes, with white porcelain slip on a dark blue earthenware ground, or embossed in low relief. Designs were also impressed in outline, or incised, in which the pattern was obtained by sinking two or three planes to successive depths, so that different thicknesses of coloured glaze gave the pattern its effect. (These are sometimes referred to as photographic tiles.) Many tiles were decorated in the cuenca technique in which the outline of the design was lightly moulded in relief, the details of the pattern then being completed by filling the resulting enclosed areas with translucent coloured glazes. A few panels were designed in which the whole pattern was made up of numerous pieces varying in size and shape, and representing an entirely new departure in English tile work known as Opus Sectile. In addition, designs were executed in tube line. By this method the main points of the design are outlined with coloured slip and the design completed with enamels or coloured glaze. Plate 100 shows Edmund Kent at work on a tube line design.

An interesting article appeared in *Pottery Gazette* of October 1909, which described a visit to Pilkington's tile and pottery works. In it the correspondent described the works, tile manufacture, art tiles and lustred pottery and he also comments on some of the artists seen in action.

The Burtons assembled a formidable team of artists and designers, among the earliest to join being John Chambers and Joseph Kwiatowski. Chambers came from the potteries, where he had been at Doulton's and Wedgwood's as a freelance artist. At Pilkington's he was chief designer, and as such he was responsible for all the artistic work carried out at the factory. His tile

PLATE 4. William Burton from a sketch by Francis Dodd, dated 1913.

designs appeared in such art magazines as *Studio* and the *Art Journal*, and he is known to have painted some pottery although he seldom used his monogram. Kwiatkowski also came from the potteries, having worked as a freelance painter and modeller before being recommended to William Burton by Wedgwood's. At Pilkington's he was mainly concerned with the modelling of architectural faience and tiles, Plate 1. Examples of tiles modelled by him from unknown designs and painted by Miss Bradley and Miss Barlow, two of the many female artists employed by the factory, were shown at the 1903 Arts and Crafts Exhibition.

The paintresses employed generally decorated tiles, particularly the cuenca tiles on which they filled in the various parts of the design with coloured glazes. William Burton did not have a great regard for female artists, having been recorded as saying that he found

PLATE 5. Joseph Burton with his son David at the exit of a tunnel kiln.

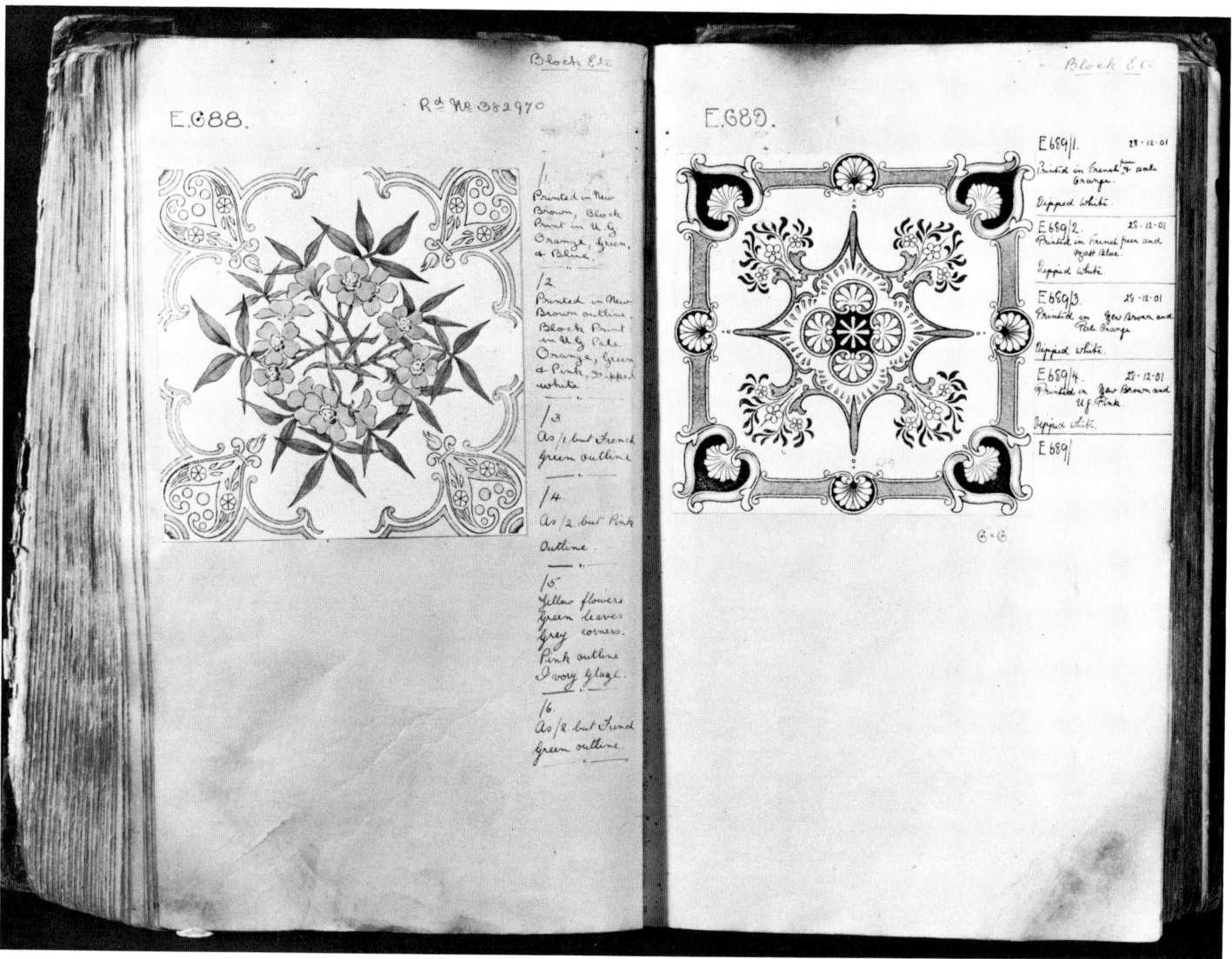

PLATE 6. Pages from a design book for printed tiles, dated 1901. Courtesy Pilkington's Tiles Ltd.

they lacked initiative and resource. Nevertheless paintresses decorated lustre pottery and one of them, Gladys Rodgers, worked in the pottery department for over thirty years producing many fine designs. Her work was always highly regarded, and in 1925 she was a gold medallist in Paris

In addition to the paintresses, Burton recruited several artists from the potteries with experience of decoration on earthenware. Lawrence Hall, William S. Mycock and T.F. Evans were the principal tile artists of the 1890s, joined in the early 1900s by Albert Hall, son of Lawrence Hall, and Albert Barlow, both of whom came to the company on leaving school. In 1910 they were joined by Edmund Kent who produced many fine designs using the tube line technique.

The Paris Exhibition of 1900 was perhaps the most influential event in the development of Pilkington's artistic products. Burton took a small party of artists employed at the factory to examine the exhibits—Pilkington's own contributions being floor tiles, wall decorations, fireplaces and hearths, with low relief, raised outline or printed designs. These were from designs by Walter Crane, Frederick Shields, Lewis F. Day, C.F.A. Voysey, F.A. Steele and John Chambers. Coloured wall mosaics and decorative pottery in various coloured glazes produced by William and Joseph Burton were also shown. The immediate result of this exhibition, apart from enabling the artists to observe the then current trends in ceramics as developed by ceramic companies on the continent, was Pilkington's subsequent use of designs executed by Alphonse Mucha. Correspondence from the Paris office of Pilkington's refers to twenty specimen designs a year and although it is not known just how many of Mucha's designs were used, four panels depicting Les Fleurs were shown at the 1901 Glasgow Exhibition (Plate 36). For many years a set of these decorated the hallway of the factory until the offices were redesigned in the early 1940's. Their present whereabouts is unknown. They were coloured in similar fashion to the illustrations of the original lithographs appearing in *Alphonse Mucha: Posters and Photographs* by Jiri Mucha

The stand at the 1908 Franco-British Exhibition was designed by two Manchester architects, Edgar Wood and J.M. Sellars. The exterior of the stand was covered with tiles developed for use on the outside of buildings, while the interior had a flattened Byzantine dome over the central part, covered with a mosaic of turquoise-blue tiles relieved by beads of silver lustre. The walls of the side compartments of the stand featured tile designs by Lewis F. Day inspired by Persian decoration, and a

PLATE 7. Page from a pattern book for painted tiles, date circa 1920.

PLATE 9. Small tile press.

PLATE 8. Page from a pattern book for painted tiles for use in entrances and hallways, date circa 1930.

PLATE 10. Sketch for a tiled fireplace.

PLATE 11. Paintress at work.

PLATE 12A,B. Panels of tiles in Persian style. These were usually designed by John Chambers.

tile panel of his design was also shown (Plate 18). The display featured a fireplace by Edgar Wood, constructed from selected marbles and inlaid with lustre tiles. From photographs taken at the time, it appears that these tiles were decorated either with a heraldic beast or a cypress tree and are very similar to the tiles illustrated in Plate 38.

The Burtons regularly used designs of three notable British designers–Lewis F. Day, Walter Crane and C.F.A. Voysey. Day's designs of naturalistic flowers contrast with those of Voysey, who executed tile designs which often combined two separate subjects, as is shown in his Fish and Leaf, Bird and Lemon Tree and Vine and Bird designs (Plate 19). The designs of Walter Crane differed again from those of Day and Voysey, generally being figure studies in stylised settings. Notable examples of his work are five slabs depicting the Senses which were shown at the 1900 Paris Exhibition and a series of six tiles known as Flora's Train, a set of which are now in the Victoria and Albert Museum. The Senses are illustrated in full in the *Art Journal* of 1900 and reproduced in plate 22.

In 1899 Day was retained by Pilkington's to design tiles solely for them for a fee of £100 per annum, with a guarantee for the company to find consulting and design work amounting to not less than £100 per annum; similar contracts do not appear to have been made with Crane and Voysey.

In addition to the designs of commissioned artists– further details of whom are given in Chapter 6– Pilkington's own artists designed and executed large tile murals from time to time. Information about these is scarce, but documentary and photographic evidence of a set of five large murals depicting pottery through the ages remains at both the factory and at the Walker Art Gallery, Liverpool, where it was installed. During World War II, however, the building housing these murals was badly damaged, but the tiles themselves were unharmed and remained intact for several years after the war until they were destroyed when the remains of the building were demolished. The original cartoons measuring 18ft × 9ft are still in the possession of the factory and it appears that seven murals were originally considered–Stone Age, Persian, Roman, Chinese, Italian, Babylonian and Greek–all designed by Gordon Forsyth in 1914, although in the final selection the Stone Age and Italian murals were omitted. The cartoon for the Persian design is missing, and it is thought that this was used as the reference for the many small prints of this design which exist (Plate 29) and was never returned to the factory.

Tile murals are extremely rare, and the small panel of a Persian falconer, which can be seen in the Manchester City Art Gallery, is a prime surviving example of work executed in the Persian colours (Plate XV).

PLATE 13. Panel of tiles used to decorate the shops of Maypole Dairies. Courtesy B.H. Tetlow Ltd.

PLATE 14. Selection of tiles in various techniques used in fireplaces and furniture.

Plate 8 shows an example of tile panels introduced about 1930 for entrance halls, and the Maypole scene, plate 13, is typical of designs which once adorned the walls of Maypole Dairies' shops throughout Lancashire and for which it is believed were painted by T.F. Evans, although none appears to be signed.

The small tiles decorated by the tube line technique and signed by Kent are extremely attractive, as are the six nursery tiles shown in colour Plate XIV which are part of a set of twelve made in similar fashion and possibly the work of Kent. They are from designs by Margaret Pilkington, who was a director of the company and a founder member of the Red Rose Guild of Handicrafts. The company itself registered many but not all of its designs and the numbers of many of these, dating from 1895 to 1920, are given on pp 89, 90.

PLATE 15. Panel of Nursery Rhyme tiles probably from a series.

PLATE 16. Tiles used to decorate a fishmonger's.

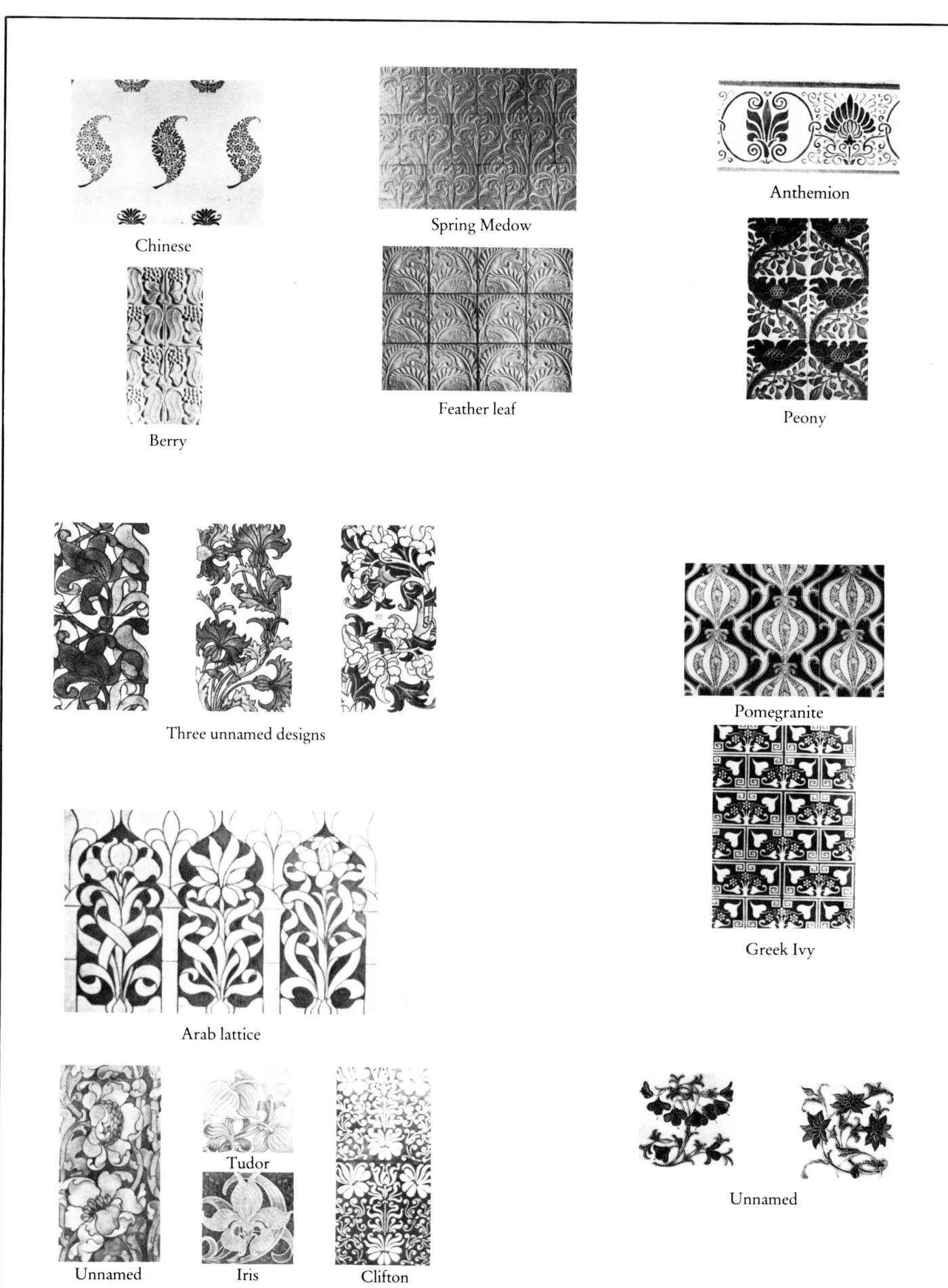

PLATE 17. Tile designs by Lewis F. Day.

# CHAPTER III
# CRYSTALLINE AND OTHER GLAZES

A glaze is a complex mixture of various silicates which, when applied to pottery and porcelain and melted by the heat of the kiln, combines with the clay body which is itself a mixture of silicates of analogous composition to the glaze.

The medieval green and yellow glazed pottery made in western Europe was produced by dusting the shaped clay with powdered lead ore and then firing it at a low temperature. During the firing lead oxide was produced which attacked the surface of the ware and gave a glassy finish once the pottery was cooled and removed from the kiln. In this way clay was hardened into pottery and glazed in one operation. Salt-glaze stoneware was produced by a similar method but at a much higher temperature, although in this instance wet common salt was thrown into the kiln at the correct temperature and decomposed by the heat. The oxide of sodium so produced then attacked the surface of the ware thus giving the effect characteristic of salt-glazed pottery.

It was essentially Burton's deep interest in the ceramic art of past centuries which prompted research to seek out the secrets of those early potters and also to develop new effects. Many thousands of glaze trials were carried out by Abraham Lomax, the works chemist from 1896 to 1911. Lomax had previously been employed as a stock clerk for the Kearsley Coal Company, but impressed William Burton to the extent that he was offered a place at Pilkington's working under Joseph Burton. At this time Lomax knew no chemistry but studied assiduously to increase his knowledge. It was an era when great advances were being made in the field of inorganic chemistry, particularly by Dimitri Mendeleev in Russia who developed the Periodic Table of the Elements. Simply, this table indicated that elements within a group exhibited similar chemical properties, and Lomax was able to use this information as he carried out the many experiments necessary to perfect new glazes. It can be said with certainty that this was one of the earliest occasions where theoretical science was applied to the art of the potter, and as a consequence many new glazes were perfected and used successfully by Pilkington's.

After the 1900 Paris Exhibition Burton expressed his disappointment at the British pottery exhibits, but he was impressed by the number of decorative methods used by the continental potters, which were either unknown or little used in this country. In 1903 the decision was taken to produce decorative glazed pottery, and the name given to this ware was Lancastrian Pottery. An exhibition of the new ware took place at Graves' Gallery in June 1904–one of the first public exhibitions devoted exclusively to the potter's art. A follow-up exhibition was held in Paris for one month in November of the same year, at Galerie George Petit, 12 rue Godet de Maevoi.

The glazes exhibited at Graves' Gallery were of four main types with variations within each group. Firstly there were the crystalline glazes which had been successfully produced in Europe and America. This type of glaze was obtained accidentally by early potters, iron oxide from the clay body being dissolved by the glaze and redeposited as crystals after the pot had cooled. Joseph Burton carried out numerous glaze trials and discovered that other oxides, particularly those of chromium and uranium, produced glazes of similar character when added to the glaze mixture. The

PLATE 18. Panel of tiles, 6×6in, designed by Lewis F. Day shown at the 1908 Franco-British Exhibition. Painted by T.F. Evans. Courtesy Victoria and Albert Museum.

PLATE 19. Tile designs by C.F.A. Voysey.

result was an aventurine glaze filled with myriads of glittering crystals, called sunstone after the mineral it resembled. The crystals contained in the glaze have the general character of the group of minerals known as micas.

A second type of crystalline glaze, in which the crystals appeared in radiating groups similar in appearance to the glazes of the continental potters mentioned earlier, was known as Starry Crystalline. This type of glaze was based on the felspathic glazes used on porcelain to which artificial frits compounded so as to be in effect trisilicates of zinc or of zinc and potash, had been added. The glaze was then fired at about 1350°C and on cooling, these crystals were formed. After an extensive research period, Pilkington's eventually managed to produce this type of glaze on earthenware at a temperature of 1000°C.

Oxides of copper, cobalt and iron were used to colour the crystals; the oxide of copper produced white needles, that of cobalt gave crystals of brilliant cyanine blue and that of iron a fine yellow bronze colour.

These two main crystalline glazes were successfully combined with the second type of glaze being produced by the factory and exhibited in 1904. These were the opalescent glazes, a more complete description of which is given in the catalogue of the exhibition reproduced pp 82-86. In his book *Royal Lancastrian Pottery*, Abraham Lomax describes the accidental discovery of this new glaze when a small quantity of a trial glaze frit bubbled over the side of a saggar and, on cooling, produced a transparent glaze containing opalescent veins. Lomax suggests that this discovery prompted the birth of Lancastrian Pottery, but it is more likely that with the Burtons' interest in decorative pottery and the factory having become economical, the time was right to develop a new venture on a larger scale. Ironically, William Burton, in his paper 'Crystalline Glazes and Their Application to the Decoration of Pottery', given before the Applied Art Section of the Society of Arts in May 1904, described opalescence as an 'irritating fault of leadless glazes fired at low temperatures'. However, he realised that whereas the potter ordinarily tried to produce glazes of uniform texture and tint, here was the opportunity to develop a new concept in glazing. Careful research produced glazes in which opalescence appeared as layers, streaks, patches, feathered or clouded colour in colours ranging from pure white or palest ivory to deep brown, orange and purple.

Crystalline and opalescent glazes appear to have been discontinued after a few years production, but the two other types of glaze shown at the Graves Gallery were produced frequently over the following years. The more important were the eggshell glazes, so-called because of the similarity in texture to the surface of an eggshell. These were matt, leadless glazes in which the active base was either lime, magnesium or zinc oxide. These oxides are chemically similar and their use illustrates Lomax's reference to the Periodic Table of

PLATE 20. The Labours by C.F.A. Voysey printed tiles, circa 1900, 6×6in. Courtesy Nordenfjledske Kunstindustrimuseum, Trondheim.

PLATE 21. Page from the design book showing two additional labours to those shown in Plate 20.

PLATE 22. The Senses by Walter Crane, 30×12in. Painted in coloured slips by John Chambers and shown at the 1900 Paris Exhibition.

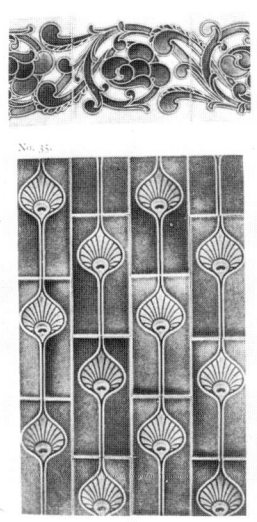

PLATE 23. Designs by John Chambers.

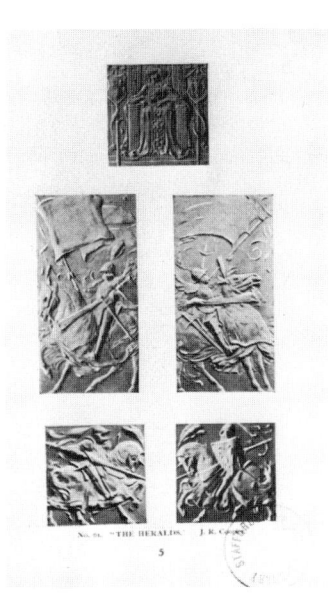

PLATE 24. Design by J.R. Cooper first shown at the 1899 Arts and Crafts Exhibition, London, see plate 14.

PLATE 25. Designs by Miss Florence Steele.

PLATE 26. Designs by a Miss Simpson and Miss Florence Steele.

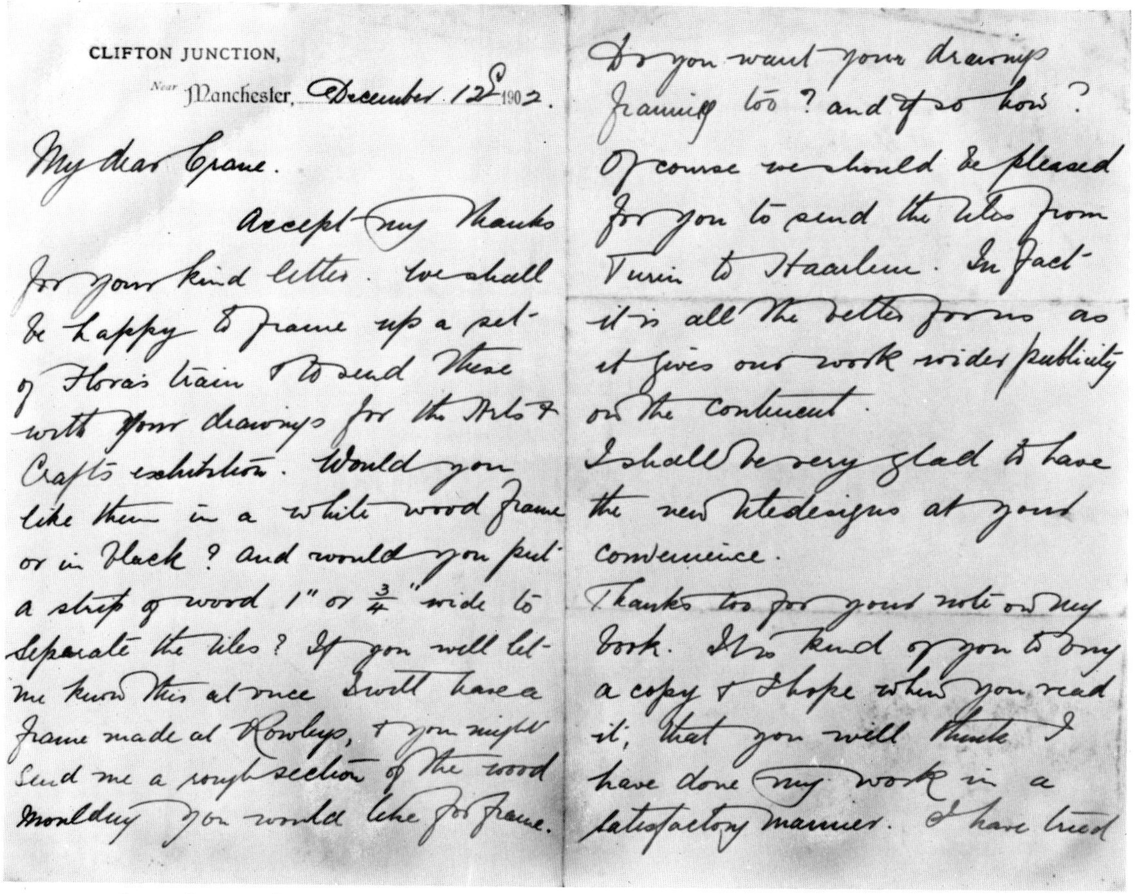

PLATE 27. Letter from William Burton to Walter Crane referring to Flora's Train tiles.

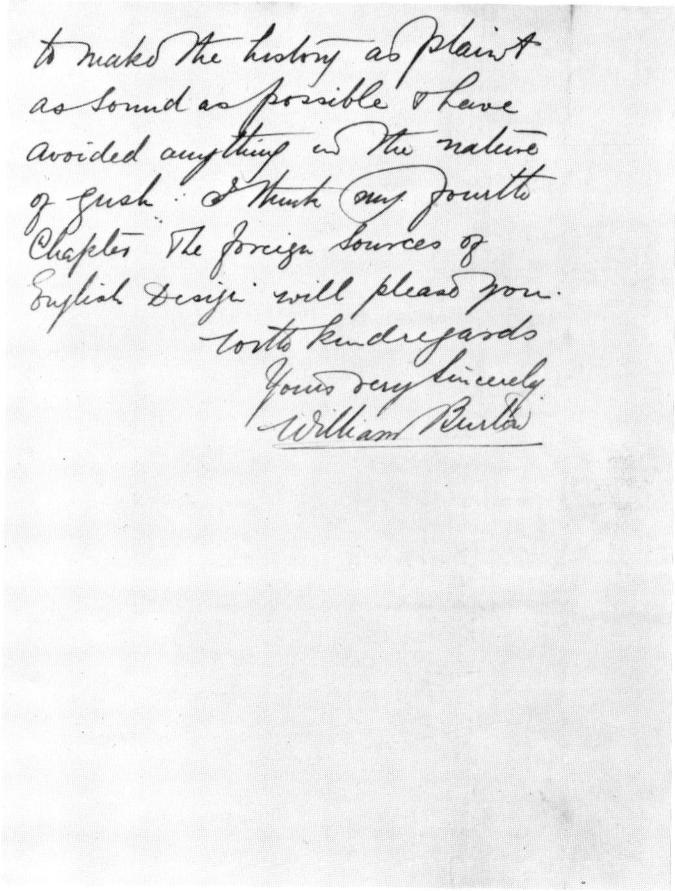

PLATE 28. Walter Crane, 1845-1915.

PLATE 29. Coloured print of the design of the Persian contribution to the potter's art. The original tile panel once adorned a stairway at the Walker Art Gallery, Liverpool.

the Elements. The usual colouring oxides were used, giving different effects depending on the basic oxide.

The final type of glaze exhibited was termed transmutation glaze, an effect in which two or more coloured glazes appeared on the same piece. Glazes were splashed with mottled reds, greens, purples and browns. A number of flambé pieces were shown where the red colour, by the addition of compounds of tin or iron, was splashed with yellow, grey and purple. Effects similar to this were also produced by Bernard Moore, and by W. Howson-Taylor on his Ruskin Pottery.

From this series of glazes three others of significance developed which greatly assisted the sales of the pottery. The first of these was known as Kingfisher Blue, which was obtained by modifying the impressive Ultramarine Blue produced by the addition of cobalt oxide to a zinc eggshell glaze. This colour was so dominant that it was found necessary to dull its brilliance by the addition of a green glaze, the resulting effect being given the name of Kingfisher Blue which proved to be extremely popular.

It was found during experiments that the glaze used to produce an uranium sunstone, if allowed to stand, separated into two distinct layers, the bottom one giving an extremely fine orange glaze. Further experiments were carried out and an uranium glaze perfected which gave a rich orange colour, subsequently known as Uranium Orange. This was a completely new effect, and its discovery prompted further experiments resulting in the well-known Orange Vermilion glaze, in which tiny tangerine speckles appear on an orange ground.

On 12 January 1912 Lomax addressed the English Ceramic Society on the subject of transparent tin-oxide glazes, having been introduced as a member of the staff of Pilkington's Tile and Pottery Co Ltd, although he had resigned and left the company twelve days earlier. This apparently was the first time that mention was ever made that a transparent glaze could be obtained by using oxide of tin. The discovery had been made in 1898 by Joseph Burton during his research for new glazes, and had been produced successfully on a commercial basis. The discovery was quite unexpected, as for hundreds of years tin oxide had been used to produce intense white glazes onto which a design could then be painted. As little as one percent of the oxide would interfere with the transparency of a glaze, but Pilkington's had produced a transparent glaze containing 15 percent tin oxide and Burton himself used a glaze containing 8 percent for many years.

This type of glaze was prepared mainly from sodium bicarbonate, fused borax, precipitated calcium carbonate, boracic acid, finely ground calcined flint and

PLATE 30. Jig shaping room.

PLATE 31. The potter E.T. Radford at work.

oxide of tin. Experiments proved that the substitution of sodium by calcium in the glaze formulation reduced the amount of tin absorbed into transparent combination.

Many examples of this type of glaze have been noted, generally with the main design in underglaze blue on a light brown ground. Sometimes the glaze itself is slightly milky with the design showing through rather faintly which gives a subdued effect and may possibly have given Joseph Burton the idea for lapis ware. Plate 42.

Between 1911 and 1927 hardly any research was carried out in the development of new glazes. This was changed by the arrival of the new chemist Arthur Chambers who produced a series of self-mottling glazes, given the name Cunian. These could also be termed transmutation glazes similar in effect to those mentioned earlier. The mottling was produced by spraying the pot with a titanium glaze, covering this with a zinc eggshell and then firing. Either or both of these glazes could be coloured using the conventional manganese, iron, cobalt or copper stains.

The introduction of Cunian was soon followed by a new type of glaze decoration given the name Lapis due to the resemblance to Lapis Lazuli. It was first shown at the 1929 British Industries Fair where it was a great success. The effect was produced by using underglaze colours covered by a lime eggshell glaze, the colours diffusing through the glaze producing a design which had no sharp edges. Prior to the introduction of this effect, potters had endeavoured to prepare underglaze colours which did not interact with the covering glaze, so that the decoration remained fixed and definite but Joseph Burton carried out experiments to produce the opposite effect; a series of underglaze colours which reacted considerably with the clay body and the glaze. The reactions tended to give soft and blurred, and broken and texture effects which were partly determined by the flow and drag of the glaze which itself depended on the shape of the pot. Artists decorating pottery with this technique had to execute designs so that the flow of the glaze and the blurring of the colour did not destroy or unduly distort their work. Simple broad brushwork patterns were used which conformed to the shape giving it added value and quality. Examples of this type of decoration are shown in Plate 49.

Although the volume of decorative pottery manufactured during the post-war period was small compared with the pre-war era, many interesting glaze effects were produced. There was, for example, a lustre glaze obtained by mixing either copper carbonate or silver nitrate into the glaze, which gave a simple all-over effect. Pots coated with this were fired in a glost oven, then removed and refired in a reducing atmosphere. Very few lustre pieces were produced in this way and examples are rare.

An interesting glaze effect is shown in Plate 123. This was obtained by covering the piece with a pattern of dots of tin-loaded alkaline glaze, over which was sprayed a fritted lead glaze containing titanium dioxide, more commonly known as rutile. During the subsequent firing, the latter glaze melted and ran down the side of the pot reacting with the alkaline glaze beneath to give the 'feathered' effect. Many experients were carried out before the conditions which produced the desired length of 'tail' were achieved.

The decoration of bowls designed by Mitzi Cunliffe posed a special problem for glazing. The bowls were decorated with an eggshell black exterior, white edge and coloured interior. For economic reasons it was required that only one glaze firing take place, the difficulty was, therefore, to perfect a white glaze which did not have an affinity for the others, but eventually, after many trials, a successful result was achieved.

All the glazes mentioned were developed and prepared by Pilkington's from basic materials supplied by Wengers Ltd of Stoke-on-Trent, whereas the new pottery made since 1972 was glazed with standard glaze mixtures obtained commercially.

The true beauty of the effects of glaze-only decoration is best shown in colour. Plates XVII, XVIII. Coloured illustrations are also shown in Lomax's book *Royal Lancastrian Pottery*, in the brochure on the first exhibition of Lancastrian Pottery and the *Studio Year Books*. Actual examples of both glaze and lustre decoration can be seen in the collections of the libraries, museums and art galleries to whom acknowledgement has been given.

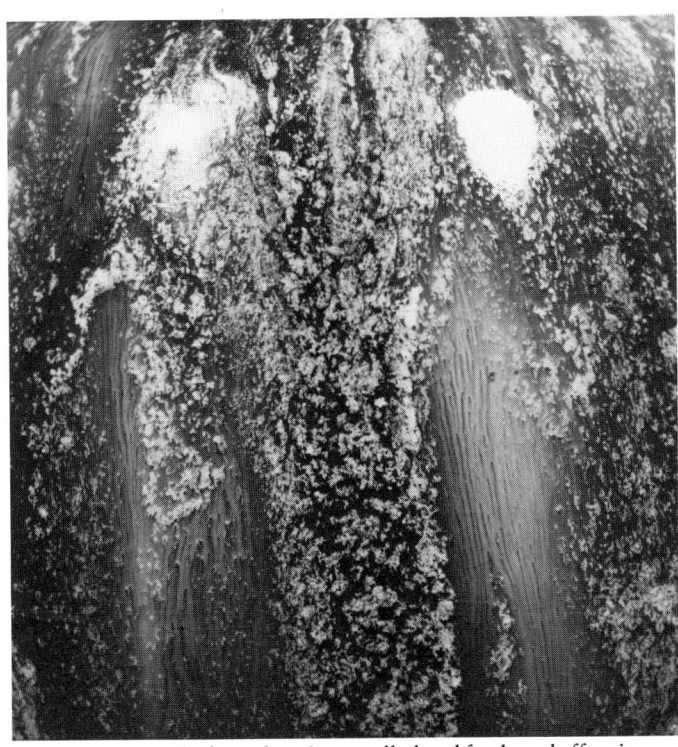

PLATE 32. Detail of pot showing curdled and feathered effect in an opalescent glaze.

PLATE 33. Slab (18×12in) decorated in tubeline and coloured slips, circa 1918. Courtesy Pilkington's Tiles Ltd.

# CHAPTER IV
# THE SPREAD OF LUSTRE POTTERY AND ITS USE BY PILKINGTON'S

The technique of lustring probably had its origins in pre-Islamic Egypt, where examples of it appear on glass. On the earliest lustre pottery the colour range was very wide, varying from vivid ruby through shades of brown to chartreuse and lemon. As time went by, the colour range became more and more restricted until by the end of the tenth century it was reduced to brown or yellow. The technique was used in Mesopotamia in the ninth and tenth centuries to decorate tiles and functional pottery.

Artists from Mesopotamia settled in Egypt at Fustat (old Cairo) and Behnasa and took with them the techniques of lustre painting. Under the Fatimid Dynasty (969-1171) lustre pottery became fashionable with fantastic birds, animals and human figures being the most popular subjects and executed in lustre of greenish gold.

With the fall of the Fatimids, the lustre painters appear to have returned to Mesopotamia and Iran. Lustreware is known to have been produced in several places, namely Rayy, Kashan, Sava, Raqqa and the Sultanabad area. Specimens of lustre pottery decorated in a style which resembles pottery from other centres have also been found at Gurgan. The design of early pieces of this period–the twelfth and fourteenth centuries–shows evidence of Fatimid taste, while a change in technique, from lustring the decoration (evident on pieces of the earlier period) to painting the background and leaving the decoration in reserve, occurred.

It is readily apparent that the decorators at Pilkington's were greatly influenced by the style of designs used by the medieval lustre painters of the Middle East–for example the characteristic cypress trees appearing on Sava wares figure greatly in Pilkington's designs. Indeed, the jugs illustrated in Plates 52 and 53 bear a startling resemblance, although they were made 600 years apart!

Following the Mongol invasion, the production of lustre pottery was abandoned in several places but continued in others, notably Kashan. However, as there was increasing contact with China, the pottery industry became infuenced more and more by Chinese Ming blue and white porcelain. Traditional techniques disappeared and were not reintroduced until the seventeenth century.

PLATE 34. Tubeline design in underglaze colours signed by Edmund Kent, 9×6in.

PLATE 35. Lustre tile by Albert Hall, date circa 1908, 17×8½in.

PLATE XVII. Non-lustre glazes of the type shown at Graves Gallery in 1904.

PLATE XIX. Lustre vase and cover by Richard Joyce, dated 1913, height 9in. Courtesy Manchester City Art Gallery.

PLATE XVIII. Glazes on pottery made after 1905.

PLATE XX. Lustre vase by Richard Joyce, dated 1909, height 11½in.

PLATE XXI. Selection of lustreware painted by William S. Mycock.

PLATE XXIII. Selection of lustreware painted by Charles Cundall.

PLATE XXII. Selection of lustreware painted by Gordon Forsyth.

PLATE XXIV. Selection of lustreware painted by Richard Joyce.

PLATE 36. Pilkington's stand at the 1901 Glasgow Exhibition.

During the fourteenth and fifteenth centuries the technique of lustre decorating was carried into Spain with the westward spread of Islam and developed at Malaga and Manises, early pieces showing a close relationship in design to Persian lustreware. Decoration was applied on tin glazed ware using a brush or quill. Spanish lustreware became much sought after, being especially popular in France and Italy. Designs were still based on earlier Muslim works, but a new style was introduced–the use of heraldic shields of famous families with designs which were typically Spanish. This mixture of styles is known as Hispano-Moresque. Towards the end of the fifteenth century the production of lustreware spread into Aragon and Catalonia in northern Spain (Fig 6), but the standards of quality and craftsmanship were lower than those of Malaga and Manises.

By the early sixteenth century lustring was being carried out in northern Italy, notably at Deruta and Gubbio. It was at Gubbio that Georgio Andreoli established his workshops and used decoration in relief to project the effect of the lustre.

Again, as in Persia, developments in pottery resulted in the disappearance of lustreware, but towards the end

PLATE 37. Les Fleurs by Alphonse Mucha shown at the 1901 Glasgow Exhibition.

PLATE 38A,B. Two 6×6in lustre tiles from the fireplace shown in plate 39.

PLATE 39. Pilkington's stand at the 1908 Franco-British Exhibition in London.

PLATE XXV. Designed to commemorate the first anniversary of the Armistice and painted by Gordon Forsyth in 1919: the inscription reads 'If it had not been for the Lord who was on our side, now may Israel say who was on our side when men rose up against us'. Dated inside rim 11th Nov. 1919, diameter 16¼in. Courtesy Manchester City Art Gallery.

PLATE XXVI. Lustre vases by William S. Mycock (left) and Richard Joyce, dated 1908, height of tallest 8in.

PLATE XXVII. Lustreware by Gladys Rodgers, dated 1907-circa 1920, height of tallest 6 in.

PLATE XXVIII. Lustreware by Annie Burton, dated 1907-1913, height of tallest 5¼ in.

PLATE XXIX. Lustreware by Jessie Jones, circa 1908, height of tallest 5¼ in.

PLATE XXX. Lustreware by Dorothy Dacre, circa 1908, height of tallest 5¼ in.

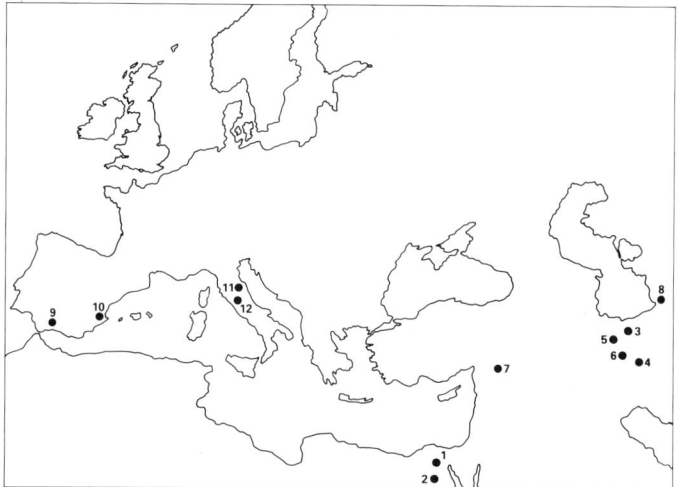

Fig. 6. The Middle East and Europe showing the centres of manufacture of lustre pottery: 1. Fustat; 2. Behnasa; 3. Rayy; 4. Kashan; 5. Sava; 6. Sultanabad; 7. Raqqa; 8. Gurgan; 9. Malaga; 10. Manises; 11. Gubbio; 12. Deruta.

of the eighteenth century it was being introduced in Staffordshire and lustring was also carried out at Leeds from about 1815 onwards, although this was not produced by a reducing atmosphere as were earlier lustres. A reducing atmosphere—one in which the oxygen has been burnt up—has the property of breaking down the compounds of silver, copper and gold which are used for lustring and thus reducing them to their metallic state in which they are deposited on the surface of the vessel being fired. The method now used was to dissolve the metal in acid, form a flux and paint the pot with this mixture. In the subsequent firing a metallic finish was produced. The two main types of lustre used were a silver, obtained from platinum, and a pink obtained from gold. Designs were mainly done by resist method.

In the second half of the nineteenth century a new interest was taken in the decorative arts, and there was an increasing tendency to revert to historical types of pottery. Hispano-Moresque work of the fifteenth and sixteenth centuries was reproduced in Spain by Escofet Fortuny of Madrid. Elsewhere in Europe lustre-decorated pottery was being produced by Zolnay in Hungary, Clement Massier in France, Maximilian von Heider in Schongau, Bavaria, Ginori and Cantagalli in Florence and Hermann A. Kahler in Denmark. In Britain the arts and crafts movement was flourishing and a new interest was being taken in art and studio pottery. Artist pottery was being made in London by Doulton, the Martin brothers and William De Morgan, whose pots were decorated either in blue and green 'Persian' colours or lustre produced by the traditional method. Wedgwood's too made lustreware from 1914, the designs painted in underglaze colours which were then covered with a lead glaze and fired. The background to the design was mottled, and a lustre which matched this was then applied and fired. The design outline was then gilded. Elsewhere decorative earthenwares were being produced by Linthorpe, C.H. Brannam, Della Robbia, Bernard Moore, Maws and many others.

In the early years of the twentieth century pottery decorated solely by glaze effects was popular and the foremost manufacturers were W. Howson-Taylor with his Ruskin Pottery, Bernard Moore and the Pilkington factory. The first large exhibition of Pilkington's Lancastrian Pottery was at Graves' Gallery London in 1904, although several examples had been exhibited at the 1896 Arts and Crafts Exhibition and the 1900 Paris Exhibition. So far as is known, the first Pilkington lustreware produced by traditional methods to be exhibited, was shown at the London 1906 Arts and Crafts Exhibition.

A paper on lustre pottery by William Burton was read before the Applied Art Section of the Society of Arts on 30 April 1907. In it he drew interesting comparisons between the many types of lustreware produced throughout the history of pottery.

At that time there were two main methods of producing lustre; the old method—in which the lustre was produced by firing the pottery in a reducing atmosphere—and a method first developed towards the end of the eighteenth century and used extensively by Staffordshire, Leeds, Sunderland and Swansea potters during the first half of the nineteenth century. In this recent development, it had been found that gold could be applied to pottery by mixing a solution of the metal in aqua regia with an oily or resinous fluid, so that when this was applied to the pottery and fired at a low heat a shiny golden deposit was produced. One of the first industrial uses of platinum was its application, in a similar way, to produce a deposit of the metal on the surface of the pottery. It was possible to produce a metallic lustre without a reducing atmosphere for two reasons; firstly, the combustion of the carbonaceous material in the flux during firing provided the reducing conditions, and secondly, once the metal had been deposited it did not tarnish in air, so that this type of lustring could easily be carried out in a muffle furnace at red heat in the presence of atmospheric oxygen.

The ease of lustring made it possible for the potters of the time to produce wares simulating Sheffield plate, and it is the so-called copper and silver lustres of this type which come to mind when the word lustreware is mentioned. Burton's opinion was: 'that it would be better if these wares had been described as "plated" or "metallised" pottery, so as to avoid the confusion of treating these not very artistic products as if they belonged to the same category as the splendid lustres of old time'. It must be agreed that the lustre produced by this method is singularly uninspiring, which cannot be said of lustre produced by reduction firing.

There is little information on the methods used by the originators of the lustre process in the Middle East, but they probably differed only slightly from those described in a manual of the Italian potters' art written by the Cavaliere Cipriano Piccolpasso Durantino in 1548. According to this, the lustre pigment was produced from a combination of red clay, copper sulphide, cinnabar and calcined silver. To this mixture a small copper coin was added and macerated in red vinegar until the vinegar was consumed. The mixture was then ground with more vinegar and applied with a brush to those parts of the design to be lustred.

The firing chamber was pierced in order to allow free passage of the flames among the wares, the kilns being only from three to four feet square. Willow branches were used as fuel and after about three hours firing, a quantity of broom was thrown onto the fire and the kiln heated for a further hour. After this time a sample was removed, examined, and firing discontinued if the piece appeared to have been sufficiently baked. When the kiln was cooled and opened the pottery was removed and the coating of clay covering the designs washed off.

This was basically the method employed by Pilkington's, and several types of lustre pigments were used among which were the following formulations:

|  | A | B | C | D |
|---|---|---|---|---|
| Copper oxalate | 3 | — | 1½ | — |
| Copper sulphide | 2 | — | 1½ | ¼ |
| Silver oxalate | — | 3 | — | 2 |
| Silver sulphide | — | 2 | — | — |
| China clay | 12 | 25 | 2 | 2 |
| Japanese red clay | — | — | 8 | 8 |

A and C gave a red lustre, B and D silver, and Firing was carried out at about 500°C.

The muffle kiln used for the firing of lustreware was quite small with internal dimensions approximately 4ft × 4ft × 3ft and was constructed in the manner shown in Fig 7. The loading of the kiln was a skilled job, the pieces having to be arranged in such a way as to allow the smoke to diffuse evenly throughout the muffle. Any spaces remaining were filled with lustre tiles. The fire was lit with the dampers at D open and those at F closed. Once the correct temperature had been reached, the fire was raked to a bed of glowing coals and the firebox filled with wood offcuts. The metal shield G was then placed in position to seal off the air supply and the dampers at D closed and those at F opened, thus allowing the hydrocarbon distilled from the wood to pass directly into the kiln.

From the many experiments carried out in the attempt to produce lustre, it was found that the heat of the kiln volatilised a particular compound of silver which penetrated the glaze giving a yellowish stain, and this was produced long before any staining from copper compounds. With copper a red stain appeared

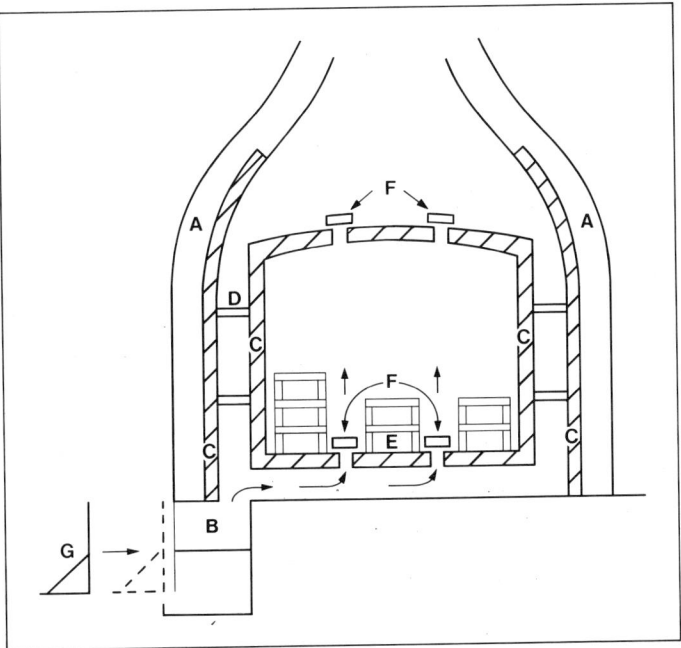

Fig. 7. Lustre kiln: A. outer wall of common brick lined with firebrick; B. firebox; C. firebrick; D. baffles; E. batt shelves; F. dampers; G. iron shield.

only when the atmosphere was heavily reducing, and it then deepened during the whole reduction time. Moreover, if the firing was carried out for a long period, the stain from the silver and copper would spread over the whole glaze surface. Staining was particularly noticeable when an ivory glaze was used for the ground.

The firing was extremely critical; too high a temperature and the lustre mixture fused with the glaze, too low and the lustre failed to develop. Uneven lustring–poor circulation of the reducing atmosphere– resulted in one-sided pots which could be sold off cheaply to the employees, but frequently, whole kilns were lost. When the firing was carried out correctly, however, the stain deepened in colour until eventually the lustre characteristic of the pigment being used was developed. A successful firing resulted in a thin metallic film on the surface of the pottery, producing a brilliant, pearl-like iridescence.

Pilkington's found it possible to produce excellent lustres on glazes of every type–leadless glazes, lead glazes and glazes with or without oxide of tin. Owing to the difficulty of the process, however, relatively little lustre-decorated pottery was produced. Up to the end of 1938 approximately 17,000 examples had been sold through agencies, and of these roughly 1,000 were sold between 1927 and 1938.

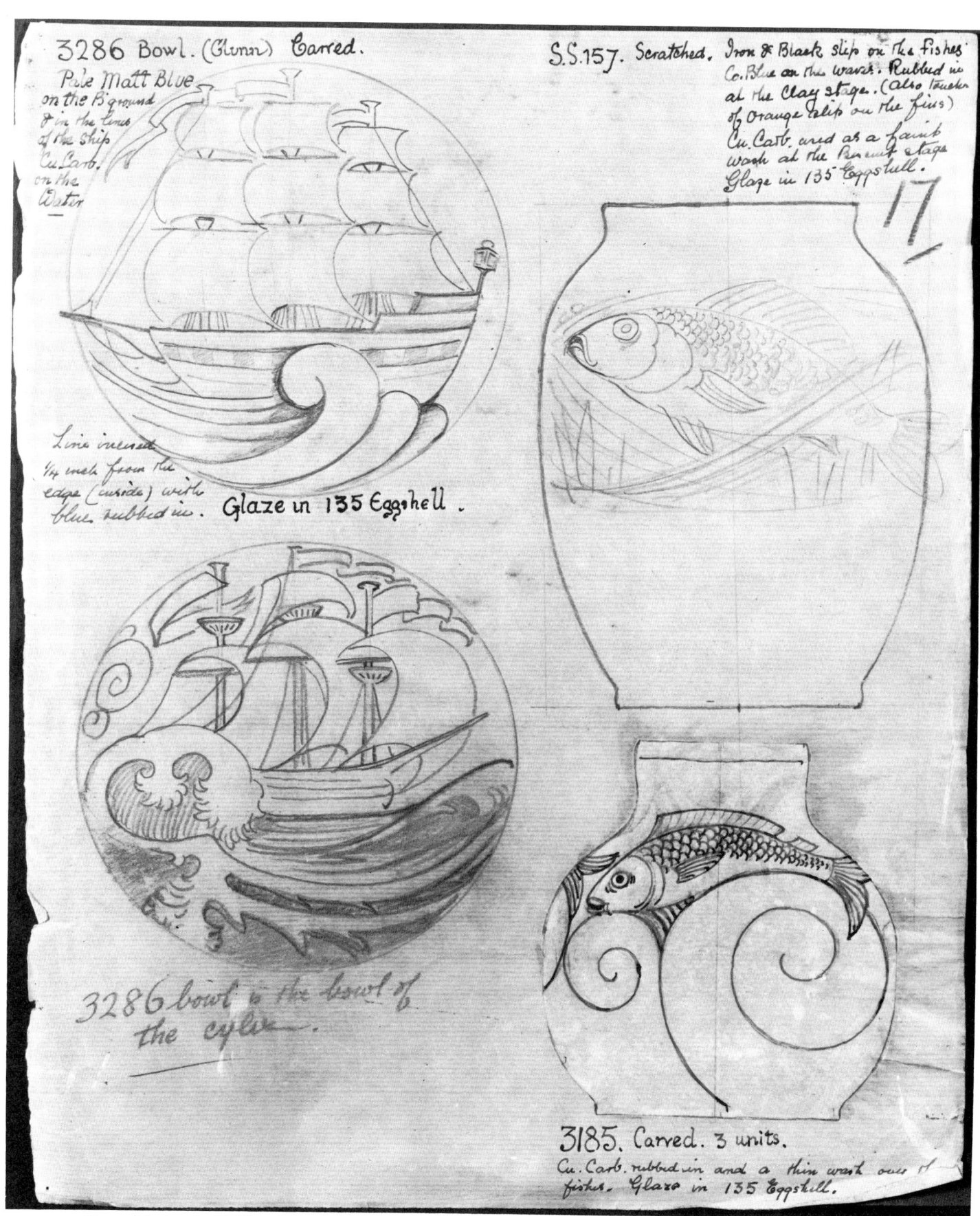

PLATE 40. Page of designs by William S. Mycock, circa 1930. Courtesy Swinton Central Library.

# CHAPTER V
# POTTERY

After about five years of tile production, the first steps were taken to form what was eventually to become the pottery department. A thrower named Robert Tunnicliffe–previously employed by Minton's–was engaged in 1898, whose duties included making moulded vases, hat pin tops and buttons. The buttons were made in two halves in plaster of paris moulds and then joined. In order to prolong the life of the moulds, clay dust was mixed with linseed oil instead of water. According to Lomax, unglazed pottery was obtained from the Firth family of Kirkby Lonsdale and glazed at Pilkington's, these being marked with the Firth family monogram. Possibly these pots were to supplement those made by Tunnicliffe, but in any event, they gave the Pilkington artists the opportunity to decorate pottery shapes which they would not otherwise have had. Tunnicliffe was given an apprentice named William Bray who came straight from school in 1900 and who remained at the factory for over fifty years, although Tunnicliffe himself appears to have left about 1908. The services of E.T. Radford, another thrower, were obtained in 1903. Radford was very experienced, having been first apprenticed to Wedgwood's. He moved to the Linthorpe Pottery in 1880, then in 1886 to Burmantoft's and subsequently to Doulton's, before returning to Wedgwood's where he knew William Burton. He remained with Pilkington's until his retirement in 1936 aged 76. During this period he acquired the reputation of being one of the finest throwers of his time.

The influence of Lewis F. Day on Pilkington's has never fully been realised. Much of the work credited to William Burton and his brother originated from Day. He is known to have executed many tile designs and advised on artistic developments, but designs by him for lustre pottery have not yet been documented, although there is evidence to suggest that the pottery shapes introduced by Pilkington's in their exhibition of new Lancastrian Pottery in 1904 were designed by Day, using as his models the pottery of the Chinese, Persian and Greek civilisations.

Walter Crane also produced several designs for use on lustre pottery (as he had done for Maws). These designs were used repeatedly up to the closure of the pottery and many examples of each design exist on pots of the same shape. Great emphasis has been laid on the fact that Pilkington's never produced duplicates. This originally referred to early non-lustres, owing to the fact that the effect of the glazes in firing was so unpredictable, but where lustre pottery is concerned, designs were used time and time again and not always on the same shape.

One of the earliest international exhibitions at which the new Lancastrian Pottery was shown was that at Liège in 1905. Here the new *sang-de-boeuf* glaze attracted much attention, the largest piece being bought by the Japanese commissioner. The Eighth Arts and Crafts Exhibition, held at the Grafton

PLATE 41. Vase, with fiery crystalline glaze, dated 1908, height 5¼in, see Appendix I.

PLATE 42. Vase, with transparent tin oxide glaze by Charles Cundall, dated 1912, height 11in. Courtesy Manchester City Art Gallery.

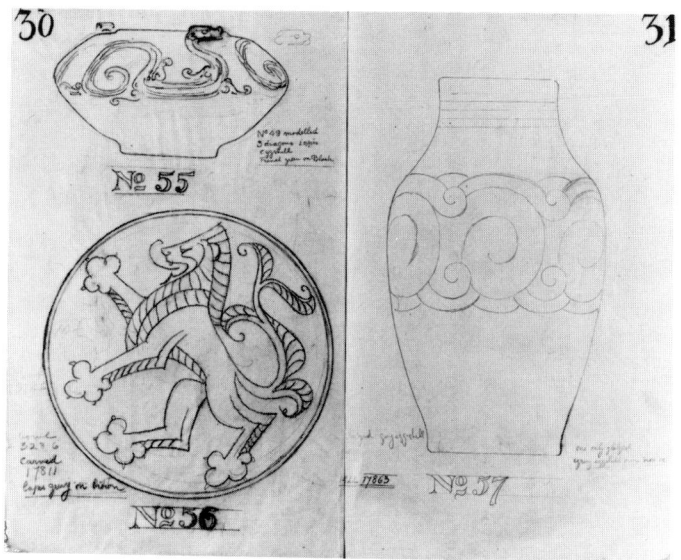

PLATE 43. Page from Richard Joyce's pattern book of shapes and designs.

PLATE 44. Plaque in manganese on orange vermilion by W.S. Mycock, adapted from Joyce's designs, lower left in plate 43, dated 1935, diameter 12in.

Galleries the following year, saw what was probably the first showing of lustre effects on forms designed by Lewis F. Day. Other pieces designed by Day, William Burton and John Chambers were made for the exhibition by Radford and Tunnicliffe, and painted by Chambers, W.S. Mycock, T.F. Evans and J. Fisher. The cheapest piece was 7s 6d, the most expensive £20.

There were also several display cases showing Lancastrian and Lancastrian Lustre Pottery at the 1908 Franco-British Exhibition, and while it has not been possible to identify any of the exhibits positively, it is more than likely that the small plate illustrated in Plate 61, the Eumenides vase and the Valkyrie vase (both illustrated in Lomax) were among the actual exhibits. Two versions of the Valkyrie vase exist; one owned by Lord Dunsany, the other by Manchester City Art Gallery. The latter (Plate I) differs in several respects from that owned by Lord Dunsany but it is apparent that the design is taken from a water-colour by Gordon Forsyth illustrated in colour in the *Studio Year Book* for 1909. Also shown were three alms dishes, possibly carrying the emblems of St Mark, St Luke and St John on the central boss. At least two series of these were made, as the St John alms dish illustrated in Plate XXXIII dates from 1909.

In 1910 Pilkington's exhibited at the Brussels International Exhibition but all their wares were lost, along with those of other exhibitors, when fire destroyed the British Pavilion. One month later, however, the British Pavilion reopened and Pilkington's replaced their lost display with an exhibition which contained at least 144 lustre pieces, including a lioness and a rat and apple group originally modelled by Richard Joyce (Plates 74, 77). The destruction of the British Pavilion had inspired Gordon Forsyth to paint a large lustre bowl depicting swirling red flames licking the ruins and carrying the legend 'British and Belgian sections burnt 14 August 1910', but unfortunately it has not been possible to trace this piece.

The following year again found Pilkington's at an international exhibition, this time in Turin. They displayed eleven stands of pottery. Some seventy pieces of hand-painted lustreware were shown, among which was a magnificent punch-bowl with a fish design modelled and decoratd by Richard Joyce.

In 1913 the factory was honoured by King George V with the award of a Royal Warrant, and henceforth the pottery became known as Royal Lancastrian.

The styles of decoration used by artists were individual to a great extent, but derived from the decorative lustres of the Middle Eastern, Spanish and Italian cultures. Designs were floral, animal, geometric

PLATE 45. Page from Richard Joyce's pattern book showing early Central American influence, see plate 96. Courtesy Swinton Central Library.

PLATE 46. Page of bird studies by W.S. Mycock. Courtesy Swinton Central Library.

and heraldic in nature, each artist being characterised by certain styles of designs. The work of Gordon Forsyth is predominantly calligraphic and heraldic, whereas Richard Joyce produced animal studies, Mycock, ship and floral designs and the female artists tended to paint floral or geometric designs. Often styles of two separate cultures were combined in one design. In the *Collector's Guide* of September 1973 a small dish was illustrated with a heraldic lion at the centre of the design–typical of Hispano-Moresque work–surrounded by a ring of the cypress trees which are a feature of early Persian lustre. Animal designs tended to be naturalistic rather than the stylised representations of mythical beasts which characterised the lustreware of William De Morgan.

Quite often the back of a plate and the base of a vase carried a design; this was sometimes the artist's year mark but frequently was an extension of the decoration. In some cases, through a quirk of the firing, the reverse design appears clearer and sharper than that which is intended to show. This decoration of the reverse is also common in the lustres which influenced the Pilkington artists, in particular those from fifteenth-century Spain.

In common with other companies manufacturing Art Pottery, Pilkington's received visits from well-known people of the day who were allowed to try their hand at lustre painting. One of these was Sir Henry Cunninghame, a civil servant and an expert on Limoges enamels and European ceramics. The jug illustrated in Plate 117 may well be the work of a visitor to the factory; it is finely painted, bears the initials A.E.P. and is dated 1912.

The golden era of Lancastrian Pottery, particularly that of the lustreware, ended, not surprisingly, at the time of World War I. The team of artists which William Burton had assembled began to break up; Charles Cundall and Gordon Forsyth left for war service, Annie Burton left to work in local government and William Burton himself retired in 1915. During the war the production of decorative pottery was greatly reduced, with only Joyce, Mycock and Gladys Rodgers left to decorate lustreware. The immediate impact of the war therefore was to reduce the volume of lustre pottery, which never again reached pre-1914 levels. This is reflected in the fact that of the hand-decorated pottery made–numbering some 20,000 pieces–approximately 11,500 had been sold by 1914, all of which were lustre. From 1915 to 1926 only 5,000

PLATE 47A,B,C. Pueblo designs by W.S. Mycock. Courtesy Swinton Central Library.

lustres were sold, and in the next ten years less than 1,000 were made; although to this must be added about 2,500 pieces of pottery hand-decorated by other methods.

The pottery was sold in Great Britain through many shops, both large and small, the most significant of which was Liberty's of London. Abroad, Lancastrian Pottery was sold by Tiffany's of New York, Nordhausen of Bergen, Desreux of Brussels and many others.

The period following the war saw not only a decline in the quantity of pottery produced, but also a deterioration in the quality, although some fine specimens were produced from time to time. The reasons for the slump appear to be fairly plain. Firstly, from the end of 1911–when the chemist Abraham Lomax left–until 1928, little or no research was done into developing new glazes and effects. Secondly, the economic climate following the war was such that a market for quality decorative pottery could not be sustained. A third factor was William Burton's retirement, which gave added responsibility to his brother Joseph who then had to devote more and more time to the company's main industry and correspondingly less to the pottery. Finally the team of artists who had, over a period of ten years, made the name of Pilkington's Lancastrian synonymous with all that is best in pottery, had broken up as already described.

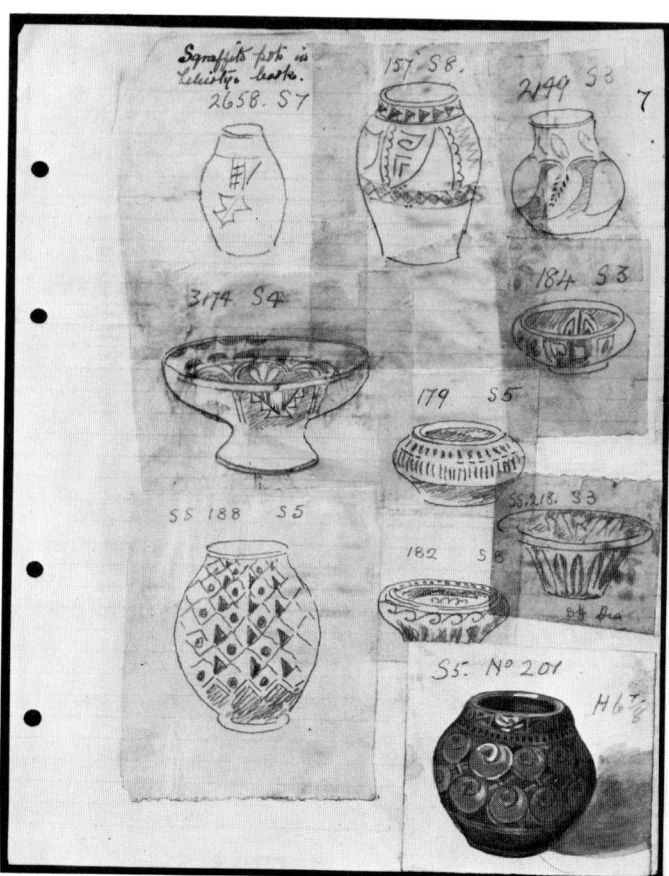

PLATE 48. Sketches of shapes and designs for Liberty's Catalogue. Courtesy Swinton Central Library.

In August 1927 a new chemist, Arthur Chambers, son of the firm's chief designer, joined the company. Chambers joined Pilkington's after spending four years at North Staffordshire Technical College, where he had studied pottery, and at once he commenced working on the development of new glazes. He successfully produced a new range of Cunian glazes, and in 1929 the pottery department was revitalised by the first public showing of the new lapis ware at the British Industries Fair. (Both these glaze effects are explained fully in Chapter III).

By 1930 the methods used for pottery decoration had changed considerably. Lustreware had once been the only type of hand-decorated pottery made, but now with the addition of lapis decoration, and sgraffito, carved and scratched designs, less and less lustreware was being produced. There was now about one lustre firing per month.

Examples of the above techniques are illustrated in the text; the large lapis vase in Plate 49 is in grey eggshell with the design in cobalt blue and copper green; the sgraffito vase Plate 111 has the design carved through as deep cobalt blue glaze to the white body, the whole subsequently sprayed with a copper green glaze. Plate XXXIV shows carved designs by Richard Joyce; these are modelled onto the vase and then covered with eggshell glazes: sometimes the designs are reinforced by colours used in the decoration of lapis ware. The designs used on the scratched form of decoration are perhaps the simplest, that illustrated in Plate 111 (back row left) being scratched into the body of the vase, outlined in cobalt blue against a grey eggshell ground and coloured naturalistically.

In 1931 the company suffered another blow with the death of Richard Joyce, undoubtedly one of the best artists ever employed by Pilkington's. Joyce was not replaced and this left only Gladys Rodgers and William Mycock to carry out decoration. Miss Rodgers's main task was then to decorate the lapis ware and Mycock executed lustre and other types of decoration. However, the spark of inspiration which had been obtained from the interaction of a dedicated team of artists had gone, and surviving record books, which once described in full the decoration on a piece of pottery, now simply state 'conventional design'.

In the early 1930s the old lustre kiln was demolished to make way for extensions and replaced by a new kiln fired by cylinders of town gas. Unfortunately, this kiln could not be made to work properly, which further contributed to the low production of lustre pottery.

In an attempt to stimulate the sales of quality pottery, Mycock spent some time as a travelling salesman, but the tendency was still to produce more commercialised types of pottery. The moulded book-ends and animals of the late 1930s hardly compare

PLATE 49. Group of Lapis vases and bowls decorated by Gladys Rodgers, circa 1930, height of tallest vase 8½in.

with the beautifully executed, free-standing animals modelled by Joyce some twenty-five years before (Plates 74, 121).

Many of the animals mentioned above were modelled by John Spencer, who had never worked in a pottery. In addition to these, Spencer made and decorated a few items of pottery in the sgraffito technique, and examples of his work are shown in Plates 119 and 120.

During 1936 the thrower E.T. Radford retired, and this effectively marked the end of the pottery for, as has already been mentioned in Chapter I, the financial record of the pottery department had then already been reviewed by the directors. Pottery thrown on the wheel did not cease immediately upon Radford's retirement, however, for in 1927 Harold Thomas had joined Pilkington's to assist in the throwing and turning department, where he remained until the pottery department finally closed in 1937. Thomas had worked as an industrial thrower in Stoke-on-Trent and attended a pottery class at the Stoke-on-Trent School of Art where Gordon Forsyth was principal, and it was on Forsyth's recommendation that Thomas was employed by Pilkington's.

When pottery production ceased in 1937, there still remained many pieces in the biscuit state; these were worked upon until March 1938 when the last glaze firing took place. Pottery from this last kiln is marked with the date.

That the pottery department eventually closed was perhaps inevitable as the company had been formed primarily as a tile manufacturer, but the success of Lancastrian Pottery in the years preceding World War I was quite remarkable and reflects the economy and taste of the time. The years between the wars, however, present quite a different picture, for industrialists no longer could afford to be patrons of the arts, and tastes too had changed. Within the factory the

PLATE 50A,B. Pages from a Pilkington's catalogue showing lustreware (upper) and patterned wares decorated with coloured slip, dated circa 1920.

PLATE 51. Lustreware made to celebrate the engagement and marriage of John Yates and Elizabeth Wilson dated 1909 and 1910, diameter of plate 9in. John Yates was a Blackburn artist. Courtesy Blackburn Museum and Art Gallery.

PLATE 52. Two thirteenth-century Persian Sava lustre jugs. Courtesy Raymond Ades Collection.

PLATE 53. Twentieth-century lustre jug by Gordon Forsyth inscribed 'NIL SINE TE ME PROSUNT HONORES' height 4in. Courtesy Salford Museum and Art Gallery.

PLATE 54. Greek cup of Dionysius sailing by the master Exekias, circa 550 B.C. Courtesy Staatliche Antikensammlungen und Glyptothec, Munich.

PLATE 55. Kylix in lustre by Gordon Forsyth, dated 1906, diameter 11¾in.

PLATE 56. Page from a photographic record book of lustreware at Pilkingtons. LL 6167 and LL 6169 are from designs by Walter Crane. LL 6168 by Gordon Forsyth. See also plates V, X, 62.

PLATE 57. Lustre vase probably from a design by Walter Crane (see text). A lustre vase designed by Crane, known as Lévriers (Greyhounds) was shown at the 1914 British Exhibition in Paris.

emphasis was on economy, and the freedom of action which the pottery artists enjoyed was also being restricted. That the pottery survived for so long is in itself a tribute to the Burton brothers' technical and business expertise.

In 1948 a promising young artist-potter named William Barnes exhibited his work at the Whitworth Art Gallery, Manchester, where it was seen by the Misses Dorothy and Margaret Pilkington who were greatly impressed with the quality of the work. After discussions by the board of directors, it was agreed that Barnes be approached and offered a position as head of a new pottery department. He accepted, on condition that he was allowed complete freedom to develop his own style. It is rather ironical that the Pilkington sisters, who had been instrumental in the closure of the pottery section in 1938, were the architects of its revival ten years later.

The post-war economic climate was such that the company could not afford the luxury of a non-profitable department; the new pottery had to pay its way. After a few months Barnes was joined by Eric Bridges and later by John Brannan, who carried out much of the work. Although Barnes had available many glazes which had already been perfected, he preferred to develop new types and effects, but he was in a difficult position as there was less demand for artistic pottery than there had been for the Burtons fifty years before. In addition, the purchase tax on decorative pottery was 125 per cent and, to overcome this, production was mainly confined to jugs, bowls and beakers. By 1951, however, purchase tax was down to 50 per cent which enabled more decorative pottery to be made. The pottery was fired in the tunnel ovens used for tile manufacture, thereby reducing tile output and adding the cost of the tiles lost to that of the pottery produced.

The Pilkingtons were satisfied with the wares being produced, but by 1953 the department was experiencing difficulty in making a profit and to boost sales, it was suggested that a catalogue of cheap, easy-

PLATE 58. Watercolour design of Pegasus by Walter Crane.

PLATE 59. Lustre Moon Flask designed by Walter Crane, painted by Richard Joyce, about 1907, height 10¾in: the reverse carries the City of Manchester coat of arms.

PLATE 61. Lustre plaque by Gordon Forsyth, shown at the 1908 Franco-British Exhibition, diameter 8¾in.

PLATE 60. Lustre Punch Bowl by Gordon Forsyth, dated 1907, diameter 20in: inscribed 'God of Youth Let this day here enter without care or fear'.

PLATE 62. Lustre plaque designed by Gordon Forsyth painted by Charles Cundall, dated 1908, diameter 18in.

PLATE 64A. Lustre alms-dish 'St. Mark' by Gordon Forsyth, dated 1908, diameter 22in.

PLATE 64B. Lustre alms-dish 'St. Luke' by Gordon Forsyth, dated 1908, diameter 22in, probably shown with plate 64A at the 1908 Franco-British Exhibition.

to-make pieces be issued. This had the desired effect and sales slowly increased. Pilkington's had obtained the services of Mitzi Cunliffe, an American sculptor, who designed a series of shallow bowls of asymmetric shapes which were initially unsuitable for production in clay. Eventually the shapes were modified, production began and, in time, the bowls proved extremely popular. As orders for these and other items increased, Barnes became involved more and more with the problem of mass production and less with the manufacture of artistic wares. As an artist, Barnes found the situation untenable, and in 1957 he left the company to take up a teaching post—on the same day as an order for five thousand ash trays was received from America. Barnes's departure heralded the end of pottery production, for once the outstanding orders had been completed Brannan also left and the department closed again.

During the nine years of production, Barnes designed many shapes, decorated mostly by the sgraffito technique and depicting fish, leaves and sometimes animals in stylised form. Glaze effects were also used, as has been described in Chapter III.

As was mentioned in Chapter I, from 1972 to 1975 a new pottery was made bearing the name Lancastrian. Several of the pottery shapes used were taken from Pilkington's and Carter's orignals and decorated by glaze effects only, but on the whole bear little resemblance to earlier Pilkington glazes. Originally many of the shapes were thrown, but it was almost impossible to find competent throwers and so the majority of the new pottery was cast. The decorative glazes used were supplied commercially, the main colours being copper-green, colbalt-blue and a uranium glaze similar to Orange Vermilion, which proved very popular.

PLATE 63. Lustre vase by Gordon Forsyth, dated 1906, height 9in.

PLATE 65. Lustre vase by Gordon Forsyth, dated 1909, height 15in.

# CHAPTER VI
# DESIGNERS AND ARTISTS

## DESIGNERS

William Burton commissioned the services of three of the foremost designers of the period—Lewis F. Day, Walter Crane and C.F.A. Voysey. All had wide experience in design, were well-known figures and were eminently qualified to provide the type of designs most suitable for the sale of high-quality tiles and pottery.

There are references to Frederick Shields providing designs for the 1900 Paris Exhibition, but there is no evidence of a further connection with Pilkington's; consequently biographical material has been omitted. The work and life of Alphonse Mucha is also omitted but is well-documented elsewhere.

## LEWIS F. DAY

Born into a Quaker family, he was educated in France and Germany and worked as a designer of stained glass before starting his own business in 1870, producing numerous designs for textiles, wallpapers, stained glass, embroidery, carpets, tiles, pottery and book covers. In 1881 he was appointed art director of Turnbull & Stockdale, three years later he became a founder member of the Art Workers' Guild and in 1888 was one of the founders of the Arts and Crafts Exhibition Society. Day lectured extensively on the ornamental arts and was the author of numerous books on ornament and design, many of which were used by the artists at Pilkington's. He was also a regular contributor to such magazines as the *Art Journal* and the *Magazine of Art*.

It appears that Day made the greatest contribution to the success of Pilkington's by providing William Burton with the advice and guidance at an artistic level which he lacked, and this is reflected in his being offered a contract, the terms of which are detailed in Chapter II. There is nothing in the company's records to show that either Crane or Voysey were offered similar contracts.

Examples of the tiles designed by Day for Pilkington's are illustrated profusely in the company catalogue of exhibits for the 1901 Glasgow Exhibition, and also in another produced for an unknown exhibition, both of which are now in the Staffordshire County Library, Hanley. Some of these are illustrated in Plate 17 and show floral designs in conventional style, while Plate 18 shows a tile panel of stylised form

PLATE 66. Lustre goblet by Gordon Forsyth, dated 1908, height 9½in.

PLATE 67. Moulded and shaped lustre vase attributed to Gordon Forsyth, dated 1907, height 15½in. Courtesy William Kopner.

PLATE 68. Lustre vase by Gordon Forsyth, dated 1913, height 8½in.

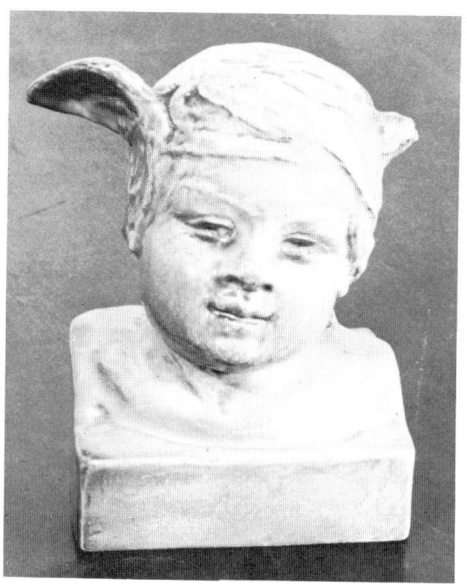

PLATE 71. Modelled by Gordon Forsyth, circa 1906, height 6in.

PLATE 69. Unusual pierced lustre vase by Gordon Forsyth, dated 1913, height 8¼in.

PLATE 72. Lustre model of a bound figure by Gordon Forsyth, circa 1908, height 8in.

PLATE 70. Lustre figure group by Gordon Forsyth, circa 1919, height 6½in.

PLATE 73 Lustre vase by Gordon Forsyth, dated 1909, height 7in.

PLATE 74. Group of Animals designed by Richard Joyce and John Spencer (Penguins and Sealion), circa 1908-1936, height of Sealion 7½in.

PLATE 75. Price list for animals.

PLATE 76. Lustre model of a pig by Richard Joyce.

PLATE 77. Lustre model of a lioness by Richard Joyce.

PLATE 78. Richard Joyce's design for a lustre vase. Courtesy Swinton Central Library.

which can be seen in the Victoria and Albert Museum. Many of Day's designs were given names and were made in the various tile production techniques available. Those known as Anthemion were painted underglaze; Celtic, Pierced, Greek Ivy and Rosace, printed underglaze; Chinese, stencilled; Arab Lattice in Opus Sectile; Feather leaf, Berry, Spring Meadow and Ogee were embossed; Renaissance, Clifton, Strap, and Nevers painted in porcelain slip; Pomegranate, Incised, Japanese Birds, Bell Flower and Sprig were incised, and Iris and Tudor were produced in the cuenca technique. There are several other designs, namely Peony, Love in the Mist, Gesso, Apple Blossom, Persian, Carved, Rosette and Coalbrookdale, but the method by which they were made is unknown.

Day also designed encaustic floor tiles and mosaic pavements but examples of these have yet to be found.

Known registered tile design numbers of Day's work are given on p 89.

## WALTER CRANE

Walter Crane made an important contribution to Pilkington's artistic development, but to a much lesser extent than his contemporary Lewis Day. Born in Liverpool, the second son of Thomas Crane, a portrait painter, he achieved fame as a designer, painter, book illustrator and writer on art.

As a young man he moved to London where he was apprenticed to W.S. Linton, a wood engraver, painting at the same time. He achieved a notable success by having a painting selected for exhibition at the Royal Academy when seventeen years of age, although this privilege was not bestowed again for some considerable time. A founder member of the Art Workers' Guild and its first president, he was also a founder and first president of the Arts and Crafts Exhibition Society.

Crane's own work was widely exhibited; his exhibition at the Fine Art Society in 1892 was

PLATE XXXI. Lustre vase and cover painted by Gordon Forsyth presented to Sir Charles Hercules Read by William Burton in 1910, height 11½in. Another version is in the Victoria and Albert Museum. Courtesy Geoffrey Godden.

PLATE XXXIII. Lustre alms-dish painted by Gordon Forsyth, dated 1909, diameter 22in.

PLATE XXXII. Lustre vase by Gordon Forsyth, dated 1909, height 17in.

PLATE XXXIV. Shapes designed and decorated by Richard Joyce, circa 1928, height of tallest 10½in.

subsequently shown in the United States, Germany, Austria and Scandinavia, and an important exhibition of his work was held at Budapest in 1900.

In 1893 Crane became Director of Design at Manchester Municipal School of Art, in 1896 he became Art Director of Reading University College and two years later was appointed Principal of the Royal College of Art, South Kensington.

In his work for Pilkington's Crane reproduced to a large extent earlier styles and designs; for example, the six tiles known as Flora's Train (Plate XIII) are reminiscent of Crane's Picture Book, *Flora's Feast*, while the Sea Maiden design appears to be taken from one of the Four Seasons—a printed fabric made by Wardle & Co, Leek, and illustrated in *Studio*, Vol II p 3. The only known tile designs by Crane for Pilkington's are the six which make up Flora's Train and five slabs depicting The Senses. At the works his pottery designs were known colloquially as Crane's Moon Flask, George and Dragon, Peacock, Sea Maiden, Figures Striped, Figures Ogee, Bon Accord, Night and Morning, Lion Bowl (Rose Bowl) and Dog Pot, all of which are illustrated in Plates II-X. A Dog Pot has not been found, but it seems likely that the piece illustrated in Plate 57 is an example of it, as the greyhound design is similar to a damask border designed by Crane and illustrated in *Nature and Ornament* by Lewis F. Day.

Recently there has come to light the vase illustrated in Plate IV in which three female figures appear with a serpent at their feet. This design by Walter Crane, does not appear in the few surviving record books of the Pilkington factory.

## C.F.A. VOYSEY

Articled to the architect J.P. Seddon in 1874, Voysey set up his own practice as an architect and designer in 1882 and, in 1884, joined the Art Workers' Guild. Initially designing wallpapers and textiles, he later produced designs for tiles, metalwork and furniture, the first exhibition of his furniture being at the 1893 Arts and Crafts Exhibition. Until 1914 Voysey designed a large number of houses both in England and abroad—usually including the furnishing—but never a public building.

He became Master of the Art Workers' Guild in 1924, Fellow of RIBA in 1929, Royal Designer for Industry 1936 and was awarded a Royal Gold Medal by the RIBA in 1940. As an author, he wrote extensively on his economic theories in relation to the decorative arts.

Several of his tile designs for Pilkington's were illustrated in *Studio* and appeared at the 1901 Glasgow Exhibition. These were known as the Vine and Bird, Bird and Lemon Tree and Fish and Leaf designs. The

PLATE 79. Lustre vase by Richard Joyce, dated 1906, height 10¼in.

tiles illustrated in Plate 20 are known as The Labours and date from 1902.

In addition Voysey designed a panel called *Lemon Tree*, comprising twenty impressed tiles, a frieze of tiles impressed with birds, mountains and ships called *The Viking Ships* and another known simply as Tulip pattern.

## J. R. COOPER

Cooper was a member of the Northern Art Workers' Guild. The tile designs by him which are illustrated in Plate 24, were first shown at the 1899 Arts and Crafts Exhibition in London and appeared in the catalogue for the 1901 Glasgow Exhibition and had been shown at the 1900 Paris Exhibition. These designs are also illustrated in the *Art Journal* of 1900 and further examples of his work are shown in *Studio*, Vol 24.

Other designers known to have worked for Pilkington's are Miss Florence Steele, J.H. Rudd and a Miss Simpson. Miss Steele was a sculptor and metalworker, often exhibiting at the Royal Academy, but of Rudd and Miss Simpson nothing is known.

PLATE 80. Artists at play. Standing left to right: Albert Barlow, Albert Hall, Gordon Forsyth, Edmund Kent. Seated left to right: Charles Cundall, William S. Mycock, T.F. Evans.

# ARTISTS

In addition to the designers already mentioned, Pilkington's own artists produced and executed their personal designs, particularly on the pottery. All the artists painted tiles while the majority of the pottery was decorated by Gordon Forsyth, Richard Joyce, Charles Cundall, William Mycock, Gladys Rodgers and, to a lesser extent, Annie Burton. Some small items of pottery were decorated by Dorothy Dacre and Jessie Jones, none later than 1908. There were other paintresses during the first few years of the company's history (decorating tiles). Their names were Ruth Tyldsley, Kate Briggs, Annie Yates, Annie Storey and Fanny Hughes; most had left by about 1905, Miss Briggs to marry John Chambers, the company's art director.

## GORDON M. FORSYTH ARCA, FRSA

Born on 30 November 1879 at Fraserburg, Aberdeenshire, Forsyth was educated at Robert Gordon's College and then Gray's School of Art, Aberdeen. In 1900 he attended the Royal College of Art, with a Royal Exhibition Scholarship, where he studied under Gerald Moira, and the following year was awarded a Design School Travelling Scholarship which he spent in Italy. In 1902 he was appointed Art Director to Messrs Minton, Hollins & Co of Stoke-on-Trent, and designed tile, faience and mosaic decoration for them.

In 1905 he joined Pilkington's as chief artist, remaining until 1916 when he left to do service with the Royal Flying Corps. In 1919 he returned and resumed his former position until leaving in 1920 to become Superintendent of Art Instruction for the Stoke-on-Trent School of Art.

During his years at Pilkington's, Forsyth produced many important and exciting designs for lustre pottery. He was greatly influenced by Persian, Spanish and Grecian designs, sometimes to the extent of reproducing the work of early masters; the kylix (Plate 55) of Dionysius in a boat is an almost direct copy of a design by the Greek master Exekias (Plate 54). In addition he designed the tile murals for the Liverpool Museum described in Chapter II. The design for the Persian contribution is illustrated in Plate 29.

Under his guidance and leadership the pottery artists at Pilkington's matured into an effective team and Forsyth's contribution to the company's success cannot be overstressed.

As a painter, Forsyth was a medallist at the Franco-British, Brussels, Turin, Venice and Paris Exhibitions. Subsequently a Fellow of the British Society of Master Glass Painters, he was also art adviser to the British Pottery Manufacturers' Association and the author of

PLATE 81. Lustre vase by Richard Joyce, dated 1908, height 8¼in.

PLATE 82. Lustre vase by Richard Joyce, dated 1908, height 10½in.

two books–*The Art and Craft of the Potter* and *Twentieth Century Ceramics*.

## RICHARD JOYCE

In Richard Joyce, Pilkington's enjoyed the services of an extremely accomplished artist who, had he been a more extrovert character, would surely have pushed his undoubted talent forward and created as great a name for himself within the industry as did Forsyth. Joyce's work–principally fish, animal and bird designs–reflect the influences of Japanese conventions, and his versatility is shown by the fine series of free-standing animals and birds which he modelled in the early years of the pottery

Born in 1873 in the hamlet of Boothorpe, near the village of Blackfordby, Derbyshire, he studied at the Swadlincote School of Art where he won, among others, the Queen Victoria Prize for Art. He taught at the Burton-on-Trent School of Art and also worked for Henry Tooth's Bretby Pottery. Later he worked for Moore Bros. for whom he painted many beautiful pieces including a botanical plate which is now in the possession of the Joyce family. About 1903 he moved to Pilkington's where he remained until his death in 1931.

During his years at the factory Richard Joyce painted many pieces of lustreware, those carrying the animal studies being the finest as they capture something of the animals' natural grace; some of them are illustrated in Plates 79-86. In the late 1920s Joyce designed and modelled a new series of pottery shapes, each of these bearing a large, incised number (Plate XXXIV); the decoration was modelled, carved and coloured with eggshell glazes.

## W.S. MYCOCK

Of all the artists employed by Pilkington's, Mycock served the greatest number of years. Commencing as a tile artist in 1894, he transferred to the pottery department about 1906 where he remained until his retirement in 1938.

Mycock was born at Handford, Staffordshire, in 1872, and during the early part of his working life he spent some years in the painters' shop at Wedgwood's, during which time he also attended evening classes. He then worked for a period as a jobbing artist among the many small pottery firms in the district, thus gaining a wide range of experience in the various techniques of his trade.

During his years as a pottery artist with Pilkington's he decorated many hundreds of pots, and, although lacking the brilliance of Forsyth and the subtle artistry of Joyce, he was, nevertheless, a highly competent artist. Mycock's own design sketches and source material are now in the archives of Swinton and Pendlebury Public Library. Many of the sketches are drawn on tissue paper, with holes pierced around the design to be used as tracings when that particular design was needed. Lustreware, Mycock generally decorated with heraldic, floral, bird and ship designs, many bearing mottos written in gothic lettering.

Among his leisure interests were music and, in common with many of his fellow artists, water-colour painting. He was also interested in literature and could quote Ruskin at length.

## CHARLES CUNDALL, RA

Cundall joined Pilkington's upon leaving Ackworth School in 1907. For some while he worked under the guidance of Gordon Forsyth, during which time his pay was 2s 6d per week! (This had risen to £1.10s per week by the time he left.) His tutelage under Forsyth is indicated by several examples of lustreware which bear Cundall's mark as the painter and Forsyth's rebus as the designer. During his training Cundall painted designs of the type favoured by the other artists but also developed a distinctive style of his own, particularly in his treatment of animal designs, which was quite different from the approach of Joyce and Mycock in that he tended to be much more stylised. In addition to his work at Pilkington's he attended evening classes at the Levenshulme and Manchester Schools of Art.

In 1914 Cundall left Pikington's and joined the Royal Fusiliers, and although Lomax states that he returned in 1917 for a short time, this has yet to be confirmed, as all the items of pottery so far discovered bearing Cundall's monogram carry the early factory mark which ceased to be used in 1914.

Cundall's ambition to attend the Royal College of Art was realised in 1917 after which he became a professional painter, and during World War II he was an official war artist. Elected to the Royal Academy in 1937, Cundall exhibited regularly until his death in 1973.

A portrait of William Burton, was painted by Cundall in 1932 and now hangs in Wythenshawe Hall, Manchester.

## GLADYS M. RODGERS

The best known of the lady artists employed by the factory, she joined the artists' department around 1907 and attended the Levenshulme School of Art. Until 1928 she painted many examples of lustre pottery with floral or geometric designs, an interesting exception being the saucer illustrated in Plate XXVII. The central

PLATE 83. Lustre vase by Richard Joyce, dated 1908, height 8¼in.

PLATE 84. Lustre vase by Richard Joyce, dated 1909, height 10in.

PLATE 85. Lustre vase by Richard Joyce, dated 1910, height 10in. Courtesy Manchester City Art Gallery.

PLATE 86. Lustre vase by Richard Joyce, dated 1909, height 8in. Courtesy Manchester City Art Gallery.

PLATE XXXV. Lustre vases by Richard Joyce, dated 1909-1920, height of tallest 10¼in.

PLATE XXXVI. Lustre vases by Richard Joyce, dated 1906-1918, height of tallest 9½in.

PLATE XXXVII. Lustre vases by William S. Mycock, dated 1909-1922, height of tallest 10½in.

PLATE XXXVIII. Lustre vases by William S. Mycock, dated 1907-1935, height of tallest 9¼in.

PLATE 87. Lustre vase by Richard Joyce, dated circa 1920, height 6¼in.

PLATE 90. Lustre vase by Richard Joyce, dated 1912, height 10½in.

PLATE 88. Lustre vase by Richard Joyce, dated circa 1920, height 16in.

PLATE 91. Lustre plaque modelled by Richard Joyce, dated 1926, diameter 15¾in.

PLATE 89. Lustre vase by Richard Joyce, dated 1924, height 11¼in.

PLATE 92. Carved bowl in eggshell glaze by Richard Joyce, circa 1924, diameter 8in. Courtesy Manchester City Art Gallery.

PLATE 93. Lustre vases by Richard Joyce, dated 1920, height 12½in.

PLATE 94. Bowls in coloured eggshell glazed by Richard Joyce, dated 1928, diameter 8¼in.

PLATE 95. Lustre vase by Richard Joyce, dated circa 1920, height 7½in.

PLATE 96. Group of vases in coloured eggshell glazes designed and decorated by Richard Joyce reflecting the influence of Central American Indian pottery, circa 1928, height of tallest 8in.

motif bears some resemblance to a Hispano-Moresque plate illustrated in an article by Aylmer Vallance featured in *Studio*, Vol 47.

With the introduction of lapis pottery, Miss Rodgers gradually took on the responsibility for decorating the new ware to the exclusion of lusteware. For ten years, until her retirement with the closure of the pottery in 1938, she worked exclusively in the decoration of lapis ware, developing a new technique of broad brush strokes in place of the delicacy of those needed for lustre work.

## ANNIE BURTON

The only daughter of David Burton, the less-known brother of William and Joseph, Annie painted a few items of pottery as well as tiles until about 1916, when she left the company to work in local government. In common with the other lady artists, she appears to have concentrated on floral designs (Plates XXVIII, 115).

## JESSIE JONES

Miss Jones received art training at the Manchester School of Art, while working for Pilkington's. Many of her lustre pots are illustrated in *Studio* magazine and that shown in Plate 116 was probably shown at the 1908 Franco-British Exhibition in London. About 1909, she left the factory and took teaching posts in India and South Africa where she eventually died. Her pots are decorated mainly with well drawn floral designs. Plate XXIX.

## DOROTHY DACRE

Little is known of Miss Dacre; it has not been possible to discover where she received her art training nor when she joined Pilkington's although she appears to have left by 1908. The majority of her work appears as small vases and covered boxes, decorated with simple floral patterns. Plate XXX.

## JOHN L. SPENCER, ARCA RMS

Spencer joined the artists' department in 1936 and remained until 1938. Born in Westhoughton in 1904, he received his training at Wigan Art School, Bolton Art School and the Royal College of Art, after which he joined Pilkington's. In the short period he was with the company, he worked with W.S. Mycock and Edmund Kent, and executed sgraffito designs and modelled figures, such as the sea-lion, and bison shown in Plates 74, 120.

During the war years he worked as an artist for Rolls-Royce and in 1949 was director of Pearsons Pottery, Chesterfield. Spencer retained an interest in painting and in 1946 was elected a member of the Royal Society of Miniature Painters.

## DAVID EVANS

Born in Manchester in 1895, David Evans studied at Manchester School of Art, the Royal College of Art and the Royal Academy School. He exhibited regularly at the Royal Academy from 1921 until his death in 1959.

His association with Pilkington's is a tenuous one for signed examples of his work are restricted to the book-

PLATE 97. Richard Joyce. The plaque on the table appears to be that illustrated in plate 91.

ends in Plate 121 and two limited editions of thirty-six–Boy and Ship (Plate 118) and Boy and Fawn, which is similar in style. A pair of book-ends, identical to those illustrated, has been found marked 'Richards Tiles', but these measure 15cm along the base whereas the originals measure 16.5cm.

## EDMUND KENT

Kent joined Pilkington's in 1910 and remained until his death in 1939. Previously he had worked for Wedgwood's where he knew William Burton. At the time of his death he was head of tile design section and was a pioneer of tube line technique, an example of which is illustrated in Plate 34.

Many of his designs were for commercial rather than domestic decoration. Examples of his work on the large scale are difficult to trace, although the pastoral tile scene in Pendlebury Library of a herd of cattle in natural surroundings and the war memorial in Albion Church, Ashton-under-Lyne, are most likely his work. Like other artists at Pilkington's, he worked on the tile designs for the ill-fated Titanic. A panel of tiles designed by Gordon Forsyth and painted by Kent was exhibited at the 1910 Arts and Crafts Exhibition (Catalogue No 272).

PLATE 98. William S. Mycock and Mary McLoughlin, paintress, circa 1936.

PLATE 99. Gladys Rodgers.

## LAWRENCE AND ALBERT HALL

Lawrence Hall was formerly employed at Minton's as an artist, and signed examples of his work there can be found. He joined Pilkington's in 1894 and executed many tile designs, some of which appeared in Arts and Crafts Exhibitions.

Albert, his son was born in 1887 and died in 1934; he received his artistic training in Manchester. His work for Pilkington's was mainly in the tile side, working in lustres.

Plate 35 shows the lower half of a tile design (the upper part comprising the remainder of a tree of typical cypress outline and decorated with Tudor roses) with Albert Hall's monogram in the bottom right-hand corner.

## T. F. EVANS

One of the earliest to be employed by Pilkington's as a tile artist, although he possibly painted a few items of pottery), Evans joined in 1894 and remained with them until his death in 1935.

It has not been possible to identify any signed work done by Evans, but it is more than likely that the small murals executed for the Maypole group of shops, one of which is illustrated in Plate 13, are by him.

The tile panel shown in Plate 18 was designed by Lewis Day and painted by Evans and is probably the one shown at the 1908 Franco-British Exhibition. A small group of tiles in Persian style, designed by Gordon Forsyth and illustrated in the *Studio Yearbook* for 1910, were also painted by him.

## ALBERT E. BARLOW

The son of a coal miner, Barlow showed much promise at drawing while at school, and after an interview with John Chambers he was given a job in the art room at Pilkington's in 1903. His first work was the mixing and grinding of underglaze colours but eventually he painted tiles. Barlow attended Salford School of Art

PLATE 100. Edmund Kent.

PLATE 101. Lustre vases by Gordon Forsyth, dated 1909-11, height of tallest 9¾in.

PLATE 102. Eric Bridges.

PLATE 105. Lustre plaque by William S. Mycock, dated 1911, diameter 15¾in.

PLATE 103. Lustre vases by William S. Mycock, dated 1912-1919, height of tallest 7½in. Courtesy Manchester City Art Gallery.

PLATE 106. Lustre vase by William S. Mycock, dated 1923, height 11in.

PLATE 104. Lustre vase by William S. Mycock, dated 1913, height 11in.

PLATE 107. Lustre vase by William S. Mycock, dated 1913, height 9in.

PLATE 108. Lustre vase by William S. Mycock, dated 1913, height 8¾in. Courtesy Manchester City Art Gallery.

PLATE 111. Group of scratched, slip-painted and sgraffito vases and bowls by William S. Mycock, 1926-36, height of tallest 8½in.

PLATE 109. Lustre vase by William S. Mycock, dated 1930, height 12¾in.

PLATE 112. Plaque in coloured eggshell glazes by W.S. Mycock, dated 1937, diameter 14in. Courtesy Manchester City Art Gallery.

PLATE 110. Carved vase by William S. Mycock, dated 1930, height 9in. Courtesy Geoffrey Godden.

PLATE 113. Group of lustre vases by Charles Cundall, circa 1910, height of tallest 10in. Courtesy Manchester City Art Gallery.

PLATE 114. Group of lustre vases by Gladys Rodgers, dated 1910-1912, height of tallest 10in.

PLATE 115. Group of lustre vases by Annie Burton, dated 1908-1914, height of tallest 8in.

PLATE 116. Lustre vase by Jessie Jones shown at the 1908 Franco-British Exhibition, height 8in.

PLATE 117. Lustre jug signed AEP, dated 1912, height 4in. The artist is unknown, probably a visitor to the factory.

three nights per week; subsequently he attended Manchester School of Art four nights a week, and during this period won several awards in national art schools' competitions; an example of the work he submitted for the 1910 competitions is illustrated in *Studio*, Vol 51. Eventually he was awarded a National Scholarship to the Royal College of Art in 1914.

Upon the completion of his training, he joined Edward Johnston, the well-known calligrapher, subsequently forming his own business, and until his retirement was a director for many years of Alan Tabor Limited, a Manchester company of designers and calligraphers.

Although mainly a painter of tiles he decorated a few pots for the most part to be shown in competitions but none so far have come to light. Few of his designs have been discovered but it is known that Albert Barlow decorated the border of the Persian tile pattern to Gordon Forsyth's design which once was in Liverpool Museum.

## WILLIAM BARNES

As a student of Manchester College of Art, where he gained a National Diploma in design, Barnes was aways interested in ceramics and the production of interesting glaze effects. On leaving college he taught art for several years before being invited to join Pilkington's in 1948 as a potter, an appointment resulting from an exhibition of his Studio pottery held at the Whitworth Art Gallery earlier the same year. The first six months were spent learning how to manage a pottery department and carrying out a few trials with assistance from some of the older workmen who had been connected with the pre-war pottery. Eventually he was joined by Eric Bridges and John Brannan. The three of them were involved in all the stages of manufacture of the pottery; designing, throwing, decorating, placing for firing, and sales. Barnes spent some considerable time in designing pieces and made the first himself before passing the design on to Bridges and Brannan for further productions; consequently signed pieces of his work are comparatively scarce. The demands of the management for the department to produce a profit resulted in a catalogue of cheap easy to make pieces which would sell quickly; this Barnes felt was a mistake as immediately the pottery lost some of its individuality and by 1957 little pottery of any artistic merit was being made although the management was satisfied with the profits. By this time Barnes was becoming frustrated as an artist and he resigned to take up a teaching post.

## ERIC BRIDGES

Was taken on as apprentice in the art department in 1936 after leaving technical college where he had developed his flair for draughtsmanship, although he had had no art training at all. At this time he had no association with the pottery, his work consisting mostly of tube line and underglaze painting of decorative tiles.

Following the outbreak of World War II Bridges' employment was terminated in the pruning of staff which took place, to reduce the number of personnel in an industry described as a luxury trade. After the war Bridges returned to Pilkington's working under the head of the design department, T.B. Jones, John Chambers having retired. The art department had been closed down completely and Bridges was responsible for its reopening, his ability as a draughtsman being of assistance in the manufacture of name panels and endowment slabs. Obtaining a transfer to the newly opened pottery department, Bridges learnt to throw pots and with his knowledge of ceramic pigments and glazes was able to make a valuable contribution to the new ware. After working in the pottery department for several years Bridges resigned for personal reasons some months before the department closed.

## JOHN BRANNAN

Upon leaving school in 1932 Brannan was taken on at Pilkington's as apprentice to E. T. Radford and remained in the pottery department until its closure in 1938. All Brannan's knowledge of pottery and skill at throwing was derived from Radford without the benefit of formal art school education which although making him equal to Radford in ability, did not provide qualifications enough for an alternative profession such as teaching following his redundancy. However, his skill at the wheel proved to be of value when William Barnes, having already reopened the pottery in 1948, was experiencing difficulty in finding a skilled thrower, and in 1951 he joined Barnes and Bridges in the making of Royal Lancastrian pottery for the second time. After Bridges and Barnes had left the pottery, Brannan carried on by himself for a short period and when the outstanding work had been completed, he too left.

PLATE 118. Figure by David Evans, No. 22 from a limited edition of 36, dated 1929, height 9¼in.

PLATE 119. Sgraffito vase by John Spencer, circa 1936, height 5in.

PLATE 121A,B. Bookends, decorated in various glazes. The Boy on Donkey pair are signed by David Evans, circa 1936.

PLATE 120. Designed by John Spencer, circa 1936, height 12in.

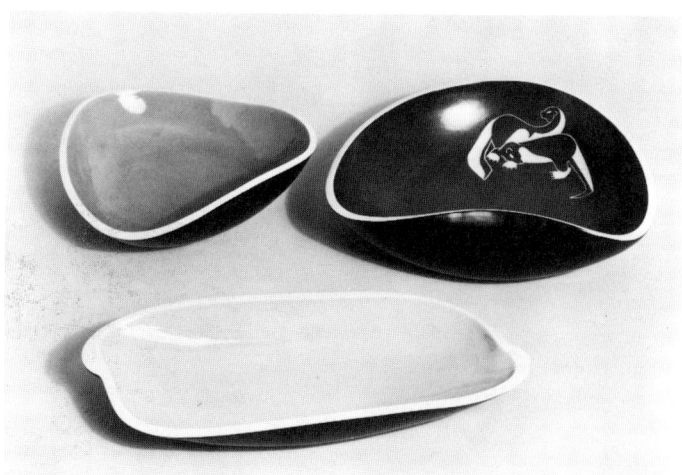

PLATE 122. Assymmetric bowls designed by Mitzi Cunliffe, 1948-57, largest dimension 16in.

PLATE 123. Selection of vases and bowls designed by William Barnes, made and decorated by Eric Bridges and John Brannan, 1948-57.

about 1900 (incised)

P about 1901 (impressed)

P 1903/4 (impressed)

1903/4 (transfer printed)

The two marks for 1903/4 usually appear together

1905 (impressed)

XI ENGLAND
1906-13 (impressed)

19 ROYAL 16
LANCASTRIAN
ENGLAND
1914-19 (impressed)

ROYAL
LANCASTRIAN
ENGLAND
1914-23 (impressed)

ROYAL
LANCAST-
RIAN
ENGLAND
1924-29 (impressed)

ROYAL
LANCASTRIAN
MADE IN ENGLAND
1930-38 (impressed)

ROYAL
LANCASTRIAN
POTTERY
HAND MADE IN ENGLAND
1948-57 (impressed)

1972 (stamped)

FACTORY MARKS

Fig. 8. The factory marks.

# CHAPTER VII
# IDENTIFICATION MARKS

From the first it was common practice for the majority of Pilkington's products to be marked in such a manner as to make them readily identifiable. All these marks are fully detailed at the end of the chapter. Early tiles were marked with a letter P, either raised or impressed, or the name of the company in full (Fig 8), and there is little to distinguish the period in which they were made other than the quality of the clay body. Registered design numbers were often marked on the tile and from 1926 a date letter and month mark were added; the key to these is included in the list of marks at the end of the chapter. Between 1926 and 1942 the date letters took the form of the name of the company–Pilkington's– and the names Joseph and David, omitting letters which were repeated. After reaching the B in Burton, the letters continued alphabetically year by year. It is possible that other year identification marks were used prior to 1926, but nothing is known for certain. Some tiles have stars or letters adjacent to the factory mark which seem to be an earlier form of dating. Some lustreware and many picture tiles in tube line carry the artists monogram.

Pottery made up to 1938 was very clearly identified by a variety of marks. These were:

(1) The factory mark (Fig 8). From a study of many pieces varieties of marks have been noted, ranging from the earliest letter P in script, to the monogram reputedly designed by Lewis F. Day consisting of the letter P (for Pilkington's) L (for Lancastrian) and two bees (representing the Burtons), and eventually, to the Tudor rose.

(2) A number denoting the shape. Pottery made prior to 1905 carried no such number, but as production increased, four-figure shape numbers were introduced. These began at 2001 and the highest recorded so far is 3258. Alternatively, some pieces which were introduced as special shapes for the lapis ware and were also used for carved or scratched designs carry a three-figure number, again referring to shape. Richard Joyce designed a series of pottery shapes which he decorated by modelling, and on these the shape number is large and heavily incised by the artist. The numbers began at 1 and ended at 136.

(3) The thrower's mark (Fig 9). Tunnicliffe, Bray and Radford all marked their pots, the marks of the two former being rather small and difficult to see. Radford's mark, on the other hand, is boldly incised. Some moulded pieces carry an impressed letter, either A B C D or E. The exact significance of these is unknown but they could refer to the moulder.

(4) A mark in Roman numerals indicating the year of manufacture of the pottery, for example VI for 1906–the first year this was introduced. The system was maintained in this form until 1913. With the introduction of the Tudor rose factory mark, the date of manufacture was sometimes added in conventional numerals until the end of World War I, when the system was discontinued.

(5) The words England, Royal Lancastrian England, Royal Lancastrian Made in England or Royal Lancastrian Hand Made in England, depending on the date of manufacture.

(6) The monogram or initial of the artist who painted the design (Fig 10). This mark is sometimes acccompanied by Walter Crane's rebus when his designs have been reproduced. Tile artists seldom marked their work but occasionally signed tiles do appear.

(7) The artist's year mark. These were used by Forsyth (Fig 11), Joyce (Fig 12), Cundall (Fig 13) and Mycock (Fig 14) up to the end of 1918, and mainly took the form of birds and animals. The key to these–if one ever existed–has been lost, but it has been possible, by means of observation and deduction, to record them and place them in chronological order, despite

Fig. 9. Left, tile marks. Right, Potters marks, of Tunnicliffe, Bray and Radford.

the fact that the pottery could have been kept in the biscuit state for several years before being decorated. The system used to date the artist's year mark accurately is based on the factory practice of dating the pottery when it was made, particularly up to 1913. By recording the year mark and the year the vase, plate or bowl was made, an earliest possible year for the design is arrived at. This, coupled with the discovery of several pieces of lustreware which are actually dated, has enabled the chronological order of the marks to be established. The one difficulty has been dating the year marks used during World War I, as examples of the pottery were not always year marked, but nevertheless, the likely order is given. Where positive confirmation of a year mark has not been possible, the date is shown in italic. As yet year marks for Mycock which could be ascribed to 1917-8 have not been found. From 1928 to 1937 he used a series of symbols as year marks; the key to these is known and is also given. From 1919 to 1927 the date was added in numerals.

There is a tendency for pieces bearing a bird as a year mark to be ascribed to a design by Walter Crane, but this is definitely not the case, as Crane's rebus is quite distinctive.

In the post-war period, pottery carried the factory mark and the potter's mark only, although some of the first pieces carried the Tudor rose and the words Royal Lancastrian Made in England. This naturally ceased when the new factory mark was designed–again in the form of a Tudor rose but simplified in outline.

Lancastrian pottery made from 1972 to 1975 also carries a Tudor rose, and to avoid confusion with earlier pieces, the new trade mark is also illustrated (Fig 8).

# DATE MARKS FOR TILES

| | | | |
|---|---|---|---|
| 1926 P | 1943 C | 1960 U | 1977 M |
| 1927 L | 1944 D | 1961 V | 1978 N |
| 1928 K | 1945 E | 1962 W | 1979 O |
| 1929 I | 1946 F | 1963 X | 1980 P |
| 1930 N | 1947 G | 1964 Y | |
| 1931 G | 1948 H | 1965 Z | |
| 1932 T | 1949 J | 1966 A | |
| 1933 O | 1950 K | 1967 B | |
| 1934 S | 1951 L | 1968 C | |
| 1935 J | 1952 M | 1969 D | |
| 1936 E | 1953 N | 1970 E | |
| 1937 H | 1954 O | 1971 F | |
| 1938 D | 1955 P | 1972 G | |
| 1939 A | 1956 Q | 1973 H | |
| 1940 V | 1957 R | 1974 J | |
| 1941 I | 1958 S | 1975 K | |
| 1942 B | 1959 T | 1976 L | |

PLATE 124. Reverse of a plastic bodied tile.

Prior to 1956 the year mark and month mark appeared together in a rectangle at the centre of the tile, the months being represented by a series of dots in two rows and the factory mark being the letter P, but it is not known when this system was introduced. From 1956 the year mark and month mark appeared separately, the months as a series of dots around the circumference of a circle and the name of the factory appearing in full.

 Lewis F Day
 Walter Crane
 John Chambers
 Gordon M Forsyth

 Richard Joyce
 William S Mycock
 Charles Cundall
 Gladys Rogers

 Annie Burton
 Jessie Jones
 Dorothy Dacre
 John Spencer

 David Evans
 Edmund Kent
 Albert Hall
 Thomas F Evans

 Albert Barlow
 William Barnes
 Eric Bridges
 John Brannan

ARTISTS MARKS AND MONOGRAMS

Fig. 10. Artists' marks.

Fig. 11. Year marks of Gordon Forsyth.

Fig. 12. Year marks of Richard Joyce.

PLATE 125. Charles Cundall's year mark for 1910.

PLATE 126. Detail of vase showing Cundall's use of a year mark as a design.

Fig. 13. Year marks of Charles Cundall.

Fig. 14. Year marks of William S. Mycock.

# APPENDICES

The following pages contain edited material published by Pilkington's Tile and Pottery Co Ltd and related to the Lancastrian Pottery. The original copy of the brochure on the first exhibition of Lancastrian Pottery held at Graves' Gallery, London, is owned by the City Central Library, Stoke-on-Trent; the remainder are from private collections.

# APPENDIX I

## FIRST EXHIBITION OF LANCASTRIAN POTTERY 1-25 JUNE 1904

In an art like that of the potter, which has been practised for more centuries than we can trace back, so much has been achieved, so many kinds of decorative pottery have been already brought to perfection, that the connoisseur may be forgiven for examining with the most critical attention any new variety which is offered for his appreciation. Remembering the triumphs of the great potters of the past, and especially of the Oriental potters of the reign of K'ang-hsi, in the production of those brilliant, delicate, or richly coloured wares which have delighted the eye of every succeeding generation of artists, it is difficult to imagine how a modern potter, working on modern lines, is to arrive at any results which shall be as beautiful as the old, while they possess, in addition, the charm of novelty. The introduction of machinery, the organisation of labour, and the force of modern commercial conditions have so uniformly resulted in the loss of all those qualities which invest the work of long-past ages with its artistic charm, that people have begun to rail against science and organized industry as subversive of everything artistically delightful. Because, during the transition period of the nineteenth century, when scientific methods were becoming firmly established in the most ancient of the artistic industries, deplorable effects have resulted by the setting up of a false ideal of mechanical perfection, it has been too readily assumed that science and art were antagonistic and irreconcilable. In truth, science, which is only another name for systematised knowledge, is the patient handmaid of art, waiting to be pressed into service, and capable, when rightly used, of producing novel and astonishing results as beautiful as any hitherto discovered. The final conditions of beautiful work remain still the same. The ancient potter, whose work we now prize, was distinguished because he used such fragmentary and traditional knowledge as was current in his day with artistic feeling, taste, or discrimination. The modern scientific potter, with much wider resources at his command, may produce startling novelties, but he can only use them aright, and turn them to artistic account, by the exercise of the same patience and the same feeling as in the past.

It seems a long day now since the streaked, mottled, flambé and other variegated glazes of the Chinese potters of the finest period were regarded by European collectors as the bizarre conceits of an outlandish people. The eighteenth century, which divided its affections between the affectations of the 'Rococo' and the neo-classicism of the 'Adams' and 'Empire' styles, has long since passed away. We are now in an age when the study of the arts of the past has advanced so far that we are prepared to recognise the artistry which often underlies productions the most foreign and remote from European tradition and sentiment. In the domain of the potter's art this is especially true, and the wonderful productions of the old Chinese potters are now prized as highly by European collectors as they are in the East itself.

Filled with a profound admiration for the work of bygone times in this direction, it has always seemed to us that with sufficient patience and industry it should be possible, not only to rediscover what were supposed to be the lost arts of the oriental potter, but even to extend the possibilities of colour and texture in pottery glazes beyond anything that had hitherto been known. Modern scientific methods have resulted in such enormous advances in every other department of industry that it seemed incredible that the old-world industry of the potter could be an exception to the general rule. Work on an extended manufacturing scale had convinced us that there were many artistic possibilities in pottery glazes that had hitherto been neglected or shunned because their production was so uncertain under modern industrial conditions that no potter could produce them successfully and carry on his business. Some of these glazes had been developed to a greater or less extent in bygone times, but in other directions modern researches have placed in our hands mineral substances practically unknown in the past.

Having produced these glazes, whether new or old, under conditions that were understood, and that could be controlled with sufficient exactitude, the problem then remained of using them in such a way as to secure artistic results. To this end we have carefully studied the idiosyncrasies of each particular glaze, and by the use of suitable and appropriate shapes, based either on the forms of Greek, Persian, or Chinese pottery, on some suggestions of natural growth, or on the forms actually evolved from plastic clay in the hands of the potter at his wheel, we have striven to encourage the glazes to develop their special qualities to the utmost. Simplicity, adaptability and usefulness have been the main considerations in determining the shapes given to our vessels. Where it was possible to make them serve some useful purpose they have been adapted to that end, and so we have dessert plates, fruit dishes, flower vases, jardinières, bowls, trays and a variety of other pieces of simple and serviceable form rendered beautiful by the texture or colour-quality of the glaze, and depending for their effect solely on the inherent qualities of clay and glaze.

In the production of fine pieces such as we now exhibit, even though our materials and processes are under such a degree of control as would have seemed impossible only a few years ago, it follows, from the very nature of the glazes with which we work, that no two pieces can be identical. In a number of instances we are exhibiting pairs of vases which show how nearly alike the pieces may be, but an examination of any of these pairs will very soon prove how unlike such likeness really is. When scientific control of material and method has been pushed to its utmost limit there will always remain the exceptional specimen which is absolutely unique, and which will be treasured by the collector on account of its rarity, as well as its beauty.

In this connection it is interesting to recall the words used by the great Josiah Wedgwood in speaking of his own productions:

> All works of art must bear a price in proportion to the skill, the taste, the time, the expense, and the risque attending the invention and execution of them . . . The most successful artists know that they can turn out ten ugly and defective things for one that is beautiful and perfect in its kind. Even suppose the artist has the true idea of the kind of beauty at which he aims, how many lame and unsuccessful efforts does he make in his design, and every part of it, before he can please himself . . . Beautiful forms and compositions are not to be made by chance, and they never were made, nor can be made, in any kind on a small expence.

These words of Wedgwood's convey the simple truth.

The wares which we are now offering to the appreciation of all those who love beautiful colour have only been arrived at after ten years of constant experiment and patient investigation. They represent the practical issue of the labours of Mr William Burton and his brother Mr Joseph Burton, aided by the sympathetic advice and criticism of Mr Lewis F. Day, the eminent decorative artist, and by the willing and active co-operation of all our working staff.

Pilkington's Tile and Pottery Co. Ltd.

Clifton Junction, Manchester
June 1st 1904.

## CRYSTALLINE GLAZES

The production of crystalline glazes has afforded, during the last ten years or so, a wide field for the display of the activity of scientific potters, both in Europe and America. Collectors are familiar with the results that have been obtained on hard-paste porcelains and stonewares at Copenhagen and Sèvres, at Berlin and Röstrand; as well as with the crystalline glazes resembling the beautiful mineral known as aventurine made at the Rookwood Pottery in America. In addition to producing all these varieties of crystalline glazes on our Lancastrian Pottery, we have succeeded in inventing and perfecting other types of crystalline glaze which are quite unique. The first of these is the Sunstone glaze, so-called because the beautiful golden and prismatic crystals with which the glaze sparkles, when it is well illuminated, give an effect resembling that of the mineral known as sunstone–a variety of aventurine. This glaze can be produced in various shades of green, yellow, and brown, which are not only beautiful on account of the crystals disseminated through them, but because they possess certain exceptional chromatic qualities which make them a welcome addition to the resources of the potter's palette. Regarded merely as colour, apart altogether from the crystalline effect, the greens, the yellows, and the browns of our Sunstone glazes have a quality surpassing that found in even the finest glazes of comparable colour produced on the famous Chinese porcelains of the past.

Allied to the Sunstone glazes is another and more striking series of glazes, which may be best described as Golden or Fiery Crystalline glazes, in which the crystals are so large in size as to be readily visible to the naked eye, and are either of a splendid flame red or of a beautiful purple colour.

A remarkable feature of these fiery glazes is the ease with which they change in colour at different temperatures of firing. At the lowest temperature at which they can be obtained they are of a splendid fiery red, so that they give to the pieces the quality of rich red lacquer or beaten copper, varying to that of iron rust. At a higher temperature the crystals become smaller and the glaze assumes a rich purple hue, while at a higher temperature still the crystals disappear, giving a subtle greenish-grey glaze of indescribable quality.

The Starry Crystalline glazes, which are so well-known on the Copenhagen porcelain, have been reproduced on our Lancastrian Pottery with perfect success. We exhibit a collection of examples with radiating groups of white, blue, or bronze-coloured crystals. In addition we have succeeded in combining the Starry Crystalline glazes with certain feathered or opalescent glazes as a background, which invest them with more striking decorative qualities.

From the very nature of the processes by which these various crystalline glazes are produced it is impossible that any two pieces, however alike they may be in form and in general disposition of colour or crystalline growths, can be identical. Two pieces may be produced so much alike as to be in the nature of a pair, but each piece has a character of its own which is unique and individual.

We exhibit four types of crystalline glaze effect:

1 *Aventurine and Sunstone Glazes*, in which brilliant prismatic and golden crystals are disseminated through richly-coloured green, yellow, olive brown and amber coloured glazes.

2 *Fiery Crystalline Glazes*, in which fiery red crystals, like fine crystals of mica, are disseminated through yellow, brown, purple, or grey glazes, in dazzling patches or in fine lines marking the line of flow of the molten glaze.

3 *Starry Crystalline Glazes*, in which the crystals appear as radiating, needle-like, or starry groups, accidentally scattered about the surface of the piece. Sometimes the crystals themselves are white–when they recall the patterns traced on the window pane by frost–sometimes they are brilliantly coloured blue or green against a background of pale lavender-blue, while at other times they have a fine bronzy sheen recalling that of burnished metal.

4 *Starry-Opalescent Glazes*, in which crystal groups of the same type as in the preceding class are developed on a background of opalescent and variegated glaze–blue shot with green, purple with brown, etc.

The general ideal at which European potters have steadily aimed in the past has been the production of glazes of uniform texture and colour. Within very recent years some few artist-potters have turned their attention to the production of effects similar to the old Chinese flambé, haricot and splashed glazes, but in very few instances have specimens been obtained whch could be described as equal, either in brilliance, or richness and variety of colour, to the old oriental specimens which are so highly and deservedly valued by every connoisseur.

It has been our good fortune, after many years of sedulous and systematic experiment, to obtain effects of this kind, which are not only worthy of comparison with the old Chinese, but which present qualities of texture, and of beautifully feathered and variegated colour, which entitle them to a distinct place among all the productions of the potter's skill.

In striving to produce glazes which should be perfectly uniform in colour, translucence, and texture, it would seem as though previous workers have neglected or overlooked some of the finest glazes that it is possible to invent. There are certain brilliant glazes, which from the very nature of their constitution do not produce a uniform coating on pottery, but one that is irregularly splashed, streaked, veined or clouded. This series of glazes, to which we have given the title opalescent, forms one of the most interesting and fascinating of the new departures that have resulted from our labours. By carefully studying the natural tendencies of each of these glazes; providing for them shapes which would aid them to break in the most beautiful manner; in a word, by following Nature's laws, we have produced a number of specimens, which recall nothing so much as fine natural products of various kinds. Competent critics have compared different varieties to finely-grained and polished woods; to polished agate, serpentine, or jasper; to the feathery moss in a running stream; and to the lightest cirri in the summer sky.

Following the classification given by the glazes themselves, we have four groups of these opalescent glazes:

1 *Opalescent-clouded*, in which the colour is broken with soft patches of opaque grey, taking on the general colour of the glaze itself in soft broad mottlings which are much more subtle and delicate than they could possibly have been drawn by the most dexterous painter.

2 *Opalescent-curdled*, in which a glaze of deep lapis lazuli, turquoise-blue, or copper-green is broken with white curds, very much as certain transparent agates are curdled with chalcedony.

3 *Opalescent-veined*, in which, by the use of suitable shapes, the opalescent separations assume the form of fine bands of variegated colour shot through the glaze from top to bottom. These opalescent veinings may be so fine and so closely drawn as to give an effect that can only be compared to that of watered silk, or they may run in broad lines of strong colour with finer subsidiary veinings between. With delicate yellow and turquoise colours, on suitable shapes, the veinings resemble those of a flower petal, while with the stronger brown and purple glazes, the markings become perfectly feathered.

4 *Opalescent-serpentine* In these glazes, besides the fine or broad bands existing in the last type, there are in addition aggregation of colour in larger or smaller spots, so that the glazed pieces closely resemble some of the finest varieties of polished serpentine, or other fine stones.

Certain glazes, apart from their colour quality, are often beautiful because of some special surface quality or texture quite unlike the uniform brilliance of the more ordinary pottery glazes. The texture of a fine piece of salt-glaze is a case in point; while the rare oriental glazes variously known to collectors as Chicken Skin, Fruit Skin, Orange Skin, etc, are highly prized for their beauty, as well as their rarity. Among our new glaze effects, in addition to the successful reproductions of all the texture glazes of the past, will be found many novel and striking effects in which the quality of the piece is determined quite as much by the beautiful texture of the glaze as by its colour. Some Continental potters, not content with what can be done in the kiln, have produced texture glazes by etching the surface of an ordinary transparent glaze with hydrofluoric acid. We exhibit a few pieces treated in this way, but the method seems hardly a legitimate pottery process, for pottery, of all things, should be finished in the kiln. That it is not necessary to resort to any such device is amply demonstrated by the wide range of effects that we have obtained by modifying the chemical constitution of the glaze itself.

The various texture effects we have produced may be grouped as follows:

1 *Chicken Skin* and *Orange Skin Glazes*, identical in texture and colour with the fine oriental pieces known by those names.

2 *Vellum* or *Eggshell Glazes*, in which the glaze surface is as smooth and impervious as that of an ordinary brilliant glaze, but the surface has only the sheen of eggshell or vellum. These glazes may be either uniform in colour or may be splashed and marked like the most beautiful bird's eggs.

A few extremely choice pieces are also shown, in which the surface texture of the glaze recalls that of old ivory.

3 *Fruit-Skin Glazes*, in which the texture resembles that of a fine pear, melon, apricot, or gourd, and the colouring varies from pale lemon to deep russet, or from apple-green to olive-brown, just as it would on the fruit itself.

4 *Metallic Effects*, in which the glaze has a texture, and often a colour, resembling that of old bronze. These glazes are further remarkable, because they are produced by an exceedingly prolonged fire, with the result that some of the metallic oxides dissolved in the glaze are sometimes segregated in shining metallic patches upon the surface.

5 *Golden Lacquer Glazes*, in which both texture and colour recall the fine golden lacquer of the Chinese and Japanese, though in every case the effect is one proper to pottery, having been obtained by the fire, and the pieces exhibited are exactly as they have been drawn from the kiln.

The term transmutation glazes was adopted centuries ago by Chinese potters to describe the variegated effects produced when two or more coloured glazes appear on the same piece in streaks or splashes, but only when such effects were produced by the action of the fire, or of the kiln atmosphere, upon the glazes. In one sense almost all the glazes which we now exhibit might be described as transmutation glazes, but we propose to restrict the term to the splashed and mottled reds, greens, purples, and browns, which differ in their composition and character from the glazes previously described. We are exhibiting, for instance, a number of flashed or flambé pieces in which the colour is due to the reducing action of the kiln atmosphere during the firing. In this way beautiful reds are obtained from oxide of copper, and by varying the composition of the glaze itself, we have the red colour variously splashed, streaked, or veined with yellow, with grey and with purple.

Purple glazes in themselves have always been highly esteemed by oriental potters, and we are exhibiting a greater variety of purple glazes than has ever been produced in the world before. Other examples of wine-purple, mulberry and similar glazes will be found among the pieces exhibited.

One of the most remarkable of our transmutation glazes is one in which splashes and patches of pink or aubergine-purple are developed on a ground of opaque green, in apparently the most capricious fashion. All the glazes of this class are so sensitive to minute variations during the firing, and to other technical conditions, that their production is attended with some uncertainty; in fact, it is hardly too much to say that the only certainty about them is that no two pieces will be identical. This is, of course, all to the good artistically, especially as the results are so far under control that the production of beautiful combinations of colour on any given piece is an absolute certainty. Here again, one of the important factors is the actual shape of the piece, because it inevitably follows that the transmutation of the colour will be most strongly pronounced either where the glaze runs thin, or where it gathers in little pools and channels. Experience is the only safe guide in a matter of this kind, and the reticent modelling, or simple thumbing, of many of our shapes has been devised so as to ensure the more perfect development of the colour-effect desired.

# APPENDIX II

## THE LANCASTRIAN LUSTRED POTTERY

The art of decorating pottery with painted designs, which shine with the iridescent brilliance of mother of pearl, or with the gorgeous effulgence of precious metals, has furnished us with some of the most beautiful and highly prized of the artistic potterywares of bygone centuries. Greatly as the art has been esteemed, both by potters and artists, it has experienced more vicissitudes than fall to the lot of most decorative processes—for it was reckoned among the lost arts for several centuries.

It is difficult to understand how, after this period of the utmost brilliance, the lustre process was entirely lost in Europe for some centuries; to be revived in our own time by Cantagalli in Florence, Massier in France and de Morgan in England who, besides producing admirable copies of the medieval work, made many interesting departures of their own. These ventures have, however, apparently reached their term too, for nothing novel or distinctive has proceeded from these artists for some years.

The new glazes of Pilkington's Lancastrian Pottery made at Clifton Junction, Manchester, have paved the way for what promises to be the most wonderful lustred pottery the world has ever seen. The lustres of the Persian, Hispano-Moresque and Italian potters were obtained on white grounds of alkaline glaze or tin enamel; either with or without the use of blue, yellow and green underglaze colours. The researches of modern science have, however, brought entirely new compounds and combinations to light, so that where the ancients had one or two grounds only, the new Lancastrian glazes offer scores of grounds, capable of developing lustre effects such as the old potters never dreamt of. The process remains an intricate and delicate one, for it demands the greatest skill to stain into an already-fired glaze a design painted in some compound of gold, silver or copper, and to produce a film of metal perfectly incorporated with the glaze yet of such exquisite tenuity that it glows with all the iris-colours of a soap bubble, a piece of mother of pearl, or a peacock's feather. No two pieces can be obtained that are exact duplicates, but every single specimen has its own especial qualities of design, colour or texture. That such a refined process should be used to artistic advantage, the advice and assistance of such eminent decorative artists as Walter Crane and Lewis F. Day have been sought, and it is certain that the vases, bowls, dishes and plaques, designed by these well-known artists and by Gordon M. Forsyth, are unique in the long history of the potter's art. Every piece of Lancastrian Lustred Pottery will bear the mark of the factory impressed in the clay and the painted cipher or monogram of the artist responsible for the design or the execution.

# APPENDIX III

### DEMONSTRATION OF THE THROWING OF ROYAL LANCASTRIAN POTTERY

Throwing is the art of shaping pottery vessels by hand on the potter's wheel.

It is the oldest method of pottery making employed by civilised man and, although the types of wheel have varied in construction, the spinning disc is an essential feature of them all.

On the rapidly rotating wheel is centred a ball of plastic clay which the thrower manipulates with his hands, first causing it to become attached to the wheel by pressure and then, thrusting his thumbs or thumb into the centre of the clay he develops a circular clay wall which spins between his thumbs, fingers and hands. As the wheel turns he draws this wall of clay into the shape required. For simple shapes the thrower's skill is such that he can obtain what he requires by hand and eye alone but, for more complex shapes, or where many are required to be alike a template of sheet zinc, thin slate or thin fired clay in sheet form is made for either the internal or external contour or shape of the pot. A piece of soft sponge is often used for shaping internally since it presents a more uniform surface against the plastic spinning clay.

Much of the Royal Lancastrian Pottery is finger-finished, that is to say, the vase is made on the thrower's wheel to the exact shape required and finished whilst it is in a soft or plastic condition, excepting for the base, this being finished later when the pot is in a leather hard condition (ie having dried to some extent) and can be turned upside down on to a clay chuck shaped to fit the pot.

This finishing of the vase is accomplished by a process of turning–much the same as for metal or wood–using a soft strip suitably shaped as the turning tool.

Some other pieces are first thrown roughly to shape on the wheel, then cut from the wheel with a piece of fine wire and removed; later, when partially dried or leather hard, they are again put on the throwing wheel and turned in order to give a smooth finish to the surface of the whole of the pot. This is accomplished by cutting the surface of the roughly-thrown pot to the desired thickness and shape by means of a steel tool whilst the pot rotates either on the wheel itself or in a clay chuck on the throwing wheel. The base being finished as previously stated.

When a turned piece is required also to have an absolutely smooth surface, the potter accomplishes this by a method called 'burnishing'.

In this case the turned pot is further smoothed as it rotates by being pressed uniformly all over its surface with a smooth and pliable steel strip, care being taken not to cut or scratch the surface during the operation.

# APPENDIX IV

## ROYAL LANCASTRIAN LAPIS WARE

It is difficult in an ancient craft like that of the potter to evolve anything really new in decorative treatment or effect, but this is precisely what Messrs Pilkington's, of Clifton Junction, Manchester claim to have done in a recent development of their Lancastrian Pottery. They have given the name Lapis to this new ware because in some respects it is reminiscent of stoneware, although the colours and glazes are softer and richer in quality than those usually associated with stoneware. Their aim has been to develop those qualities which are inherent in glazed pottery with the added charm of simple but effective brushwork pattern in the design and execution of which the individuality of the artist finds full scope for expression. Every material has its own intrinsic and characteristic properties and these bear the same relationship to the material that individuality does to the craftsman. The revelation of these properties by means of the various processes employed, gives those precious and distinctive qualities which differentiate work in one material from work in any other and it is the aim of the good craftsman to reveal them and, if possible, to enhance the value of those qualities through which he finds expression.

The processes involved in the making of pottery fall into two groups. The first of these consists of the manipulative processes such as shaping, painting et cetera which are completely under the control of the craftsman and are, indeed, his chief means of direct expression. The other group consists of the firing processes in which chemical and physical changes are brought about which are only indirectly and incompletely under the control of the potter and are, in fact, the expression of the interplay of natural forces. These chemical reactions and the consequent physical changes are not carried to completion but are arrested at the moment when the firing process if finished so that transient and elusive effects are held and made permanent. Every process may develop qualities of one kind or another, each one of which has its own aesthetic value, but the effects produced during the firing of the ware have all the variety, charm and mystery of nature. Linked up with its aesthetic appreciation, the understanding eye can see in these arrested effects something of the nature of the materials and of the changes brought about by fire—the subtle modifications of form due to contraction; the interactions of body, glaze and underglaze colour; the sluggish flow and gathering of the melting glaze and, with glazes of a certain type, the gradual change from opacity through tanslucence towards transparency often accompanied by opalescence and other less obvious effects, all of which add their quota to the complex but generally harmonious result.

In the development of the new lapis ware, all these considerations have been kept in mind and conditions have been set up which give full scope to all the factors which help in the creation of interesting and beautiful pottery quality. With few exceptions, the clay forms are thrown and finger-finished on the potter's wheel and the decoration of each piece is individually considered, designed and painted by the artist, who uses underglaze pigments of a new type especially prepared for this ware. The ornament is very conventional or abstract, rhythmic and modern, and as it is suggested partly by the pot itself, it is not only fitting but it also enhances the value of the shape. A number of new underglaze colours and coloured glazes have been prepared and these are so compounded and fired that the colour partly dissolves and softens or blurs into the glaze so that coloured glaze and underglaze colour interact and modify each other and fire to a unity or harmony of effect which is distinctive in quality and characteristic of the new ware. The glazes are translucent and opalescent with a semi-dull, shell-like finish that is pleasant to the touch and restful to the eye.

A small group of highly-skilled craftsmen carry out the various processes and each one is imbued with the same idea—the development of beautiful quality in the finished ware. Behind and through all the work is a unity of aim which co-ordinates everything to this end so that there is no conflict of effort or effect and no forcing of one quality at the expense of others or in any way that might interfere with the general harmony. How far Messrs Pilkington's have succeeded in welding all these factors into unity and beauty must be judged by an inspection of the new lapis ware, but at least a serious attempt has been made to place pottery of fine technical and artistic qualities on the market at a price that will allow it to be used for general decorative and utility purposes in the home.

# APPENDIX V

## PILKINGTON'S TILE & POTTERY CO LTD LIST OF KNOWN REGISTERED DESIGN NUMBERS

Designs by LEWIS F. DAY are shown in *italic*.

*253078 253079 253080 253081 253590 253591 253876*

*253877 254383 254384* 257472 257473 259568 259569

259570 259571 259572 265241 271050 271051 271052

271236 274178 274179 274180 274181 274886 281721

281722 281723 281724 303248 309349 309350 309351

309352 309353 310973 310974 310975 310976 310977

310978 310514 320077 325110 325111 325112 325113

325114 325115 330768 333509 334587 334588 335828

361273 365046 365740 365741 365742 365743 *365744*

*365745 365746* 366555 366556 366557 366558 373792

373793 377127 382963 382964 382965 382966 382968

382969 382970 382971 391191 397655 397656 400267

400268 400269 400270 400271 400272 417175 417176

417177 417178 417179 417252 440212 440213 440214

440215 440216 440217 440218 440219 440220 440221

440222 440223 440224 444346 444347 444348 444349

444350 444351 444352 444353 444354 444355 444356

444357 447596 448351 448723 455873 445874 455875

459943 459944 459945 462197 462198 462199 462220

467173 467174 467175 467176 467177 467178 467179

467180 469284 469285 471168 471169 471170 471171

482805 482806 482807 491137 492243 492633 492634

492635 492636 493073 493074 493474 494017 516010

516011 516012 516013 516014 516015 516016 516017

518454 518455 518456 518457 518458 519883 519884

519885 519886 519887 519888 519889 532523 532524

532525 532802 532803 532804 533205 533206 533207

534192 534193 536070 536071 536072 536073 536074

536075 536076 539278 554727 554728 554729 554730

554731 554732 554733 554734 554787 554788 562545

562546 562547 562548 562605 562606 572992 572993 572994 572995 572996 572997 572998 573636 573637 573638 573639 573640 574964 574965 576685 576686 576687 576688 576689 576690 576691 576692 576693 576694 576695 576696 580029 581505 581506 581507 581508 592537 592538 592539 592540 592541 592542 592543 592544 592882 592883 592884 592885 592886 592887 593110 595697 595698 595699 595700 595701 595702 595703 597440 611826 611827 611828 611829 612353 612354 612637 612638 612639 612640 615378 615774 628548 628549 628550 628551 628552 628553 628554 628555 628556 633219 633220 653218 653219 653220 653221 653222 656237 656238 657503 657504 657505 657506 663242

# SELECTED BIBLIOGRAPHY

Adams, John. 'Potters Parade', *Pottery and Glass*, October 1948
Barnard, Julian. *Victorian Ceramic Tiles*, 1972
Charleston, R.J.(ed). *World Ceramics*, 1968
Crane, Walter. *Ideals in Art*, 1905
——. *An Artist's Reminiscences*, 1907
Cross, A.J. 'Pilkington's Royal Lancastrian Pottery 1904-57', *Collector's Guide*, September 1973
Davis, Chester. 'Pilkington's Royal Lancastrian Pottery', *Spinning Wheel*, March 1970
Day, Lewis F. *Nature and Ornament*, 1908
Dunnicliffe, P.G. 'A Background and History of Royal Lancastrian Pottery', thesis, St John's College, York, 1968
Godden, Geoffrey. 'Pilkington's Royal Lancastrian Pottery', *Apollo*, October 1961
——. *Encyclopaedia of British Pottery and Porcelain Marks*, 1964
Honey, B. *The Art of the Potter: A Book for the Collector and Connoisseur*, 1945
Jervis, W.P. *The Encyclopedia of Ceramics*, New York, 1902
Konody, P.G. *Walter Crane*, 1902
Lomax, Abraham. *Royal Lancastrian Pottery*, 1957
Mucha, Jiri. *Alphonse Mucha: Posters and Photographs*, 1971
Rose, A. 'Lancastrian Lustred Pottery', *American Pottery Gazette*, 1908
Thornton, Lynne, 'Pilkington's Royal Lancastrian Lustre Pottery' *The Connoisseur*, May 1970

## EXHIBITION CATALOGUES AND JOURNALS
*Art Journal*
*Arts and Crafts Exhibitions*
*British Sources of Art Nouveau*, Whitworth Art Gallery, 1969
*Illustrated Review to the 1908 Franco-British Exhibition*
Mullinex, F. *Lancastrian and Royal Lancastrian Pottery*, 1968 Travelling exhibition arranged by the North Western Museum and Art Gallery Service
*Pottery Gazette and Glass Trades Review*
*Studio*
*Studio Year Book*
*Victorian and Edwardian Decorative Arts*, Victoria and Albert Museum, 1952
*Victorian and Edwardian Decorative Art: The Handley Read Collection*, Royal Academy of Arts, 1972

# INDEX FOR COLOUR PLATES

| Plate | | Page |
|---|---|---|
| I | Lustre vase by Gordon Forsyth | 2 |
| II | Crane's figures | 9 |
| III | Crane's Lion Bowl | 9 |
| IV | Designed by Walter Crane | 9 |
| V | Crane's Sea Maiden | 9 |
| VI | Crane's Bon Accord | 9 |
| VII | Crane's Night and Morning | 9 |
| VIII | Crane's Peacock | 13 |
| IX | Tiles painted in Persian style | 13 |
| X | Crane's George and Dragon | 13 |
| XI | Selection of tiles from known designers | 13 |
| XII | Selection of decorative tiles | 13 |
| XIII | Tiles designed by Walter Crane known as Flora's Train | 16 |
| XIV | Part set of nursery rhyme tiles in tubeline | 16 |
| XV | Panel of 6×6in. tiles designed by Gordon Forsyth | 16 |
| XVI | Tile Panels showing pottery through the ages | 16 |
| XVII | Non-lustre glazes of the type shown at Grave's Gallery in 1904 | 34 |
| XVIII | Glazes on pottery, made after 1905 | 34 |
| XIX | Lustre vase and cover by Richard Joyce | 34 |
| XX | Lustre vase by Richard Joyce | 34 |
| XXI | Selection of lustre ware painted by William S. Mycock | 35 |
| XXII | Selection of lustreware painted by Gordon Forsyth | 35 |
| XXIII | Selection of lustreware painted by Charles Cundall | 35 |
| XXIV | Selection of lustreware painted by Richard Joyce | 35 |
| XXV | Designed to commemorate the first anniversary of the armistice | 38 |
| XXVI | Lustre vases by William S. Mycock and Richard Joyce | 38 |
| XXVII | Lustreware by Gladys Rodgers | 39 |
| XXVIII | Lustreware by Annie Burton | 39 |
| XXIX | Lustreware by Jessie Jones | 39 |
| XXX | Lustreware by Dorothy Dacre | 39 |
| XXXI | Lustre vase and cover by Gordon Forsyth | 57 |
| XXXII | Lustre vase by Gordon Forsyth | 57 |
| XXXIII | Lustre alms-dish by Gordon Forsyth | 57 |
| XXXIV | Shapes designed by Richard Joyce | 57 |
| XXXV | Lustre vases by Richard Joyce | 61 |
| XXXVI | Lustre vases by Richard Joyce | 61 |
| XXXVII | Lustre vases by William Mycock | 61 |
| XXXVIII | Lustre vases by William Mycock | 61 |

# GENERAL INDEX

Adams, John, 15
Andreoli, Georgio, 36
Arts and Crafts Exhibition 1893, 58; 1896, 40; 1899, 58, pl.24; 1903, 19; 1906, 40, 43, 1910, 65
Arts and Crafts Exhibition Society, 53, 56
*Art Journal*, 19, 22, 53, 58
Art Workers' Guild, 53, 56, 58; Northern Art Workers' Guild, 58

Barlow, Albert E., 20, 66, pl.80
Barlow, Miss, 19
Barnes, William, 50, 71; vases & bowls, pl.123
Barraclough, J. B., 11
Bradley, Miss, 19
Brannan, John, 50, 71; vases & bowls, pl.123
Bray, William, 43; identification marks, 75
Bridges, Eric, 50, 71, pl.102; vases & bowls, pl.123
Briggs, Kate, 50
British Industries Fair 1929, 31
British Society of Master Glass Painters, 59
Bretby Pottery, 60
Brussels International Exhibition 1910, 44
Burton, Annie, 45, 59, 64; vases, pl.115
Burton, David, 12, pl.5
Burton, Joseph, 10, pls.3, 5; education, 11; exhibits in Paris, 20; research on glazes, 11, 25, 30
Burton, William, pls.3, 4; early life, education, 10; manager at Pilkington's, 10; designs factory, 10; at Wedgwood, 10; retires, 11, 45; exhibits in Paris, 20; at Arts and Crafts, 43; author and lecturer, 11; paper on lustre pottery, 40; paper on crystalline glazes, 26; letter to Walter Crane, pl.27

Cantagalli, 40, 86
Carter & Co., 15
Chambers, Arthur, 31, 46
Chambers, John, 18, 20, 44, 59, 71, pl.22; designs, pl.23
Clifton, 10; local conditions, 10
Clifton & Kearsley Coal Co., 10
Cooper, J. R., 58; design, pl.24
Crane, Walter, 20, 43, 86; life, 56; letter from William Burton, pl.25; identification marks, 75; designs, 58; *The Senses*, 22, pl.22; vase, pl.57; flask, pl.59; watercolour design, 58
Cundall, Charles, 45, 59, pl.80; life, 60; identification marks, 75; vases, pl.42, pl.113; plaque, pl.62
Cunliffe, Mitzi, 31, 52; bowls, pl.122
Cunninghame, Sir Henry, 45

Dacre, Dorothy, 59; life, 64
Day, Lewis F., 20, 44, 86; life, 53; importance to Pilkington's, 43; *Nature and Ornament*, 58; designs, pl.17; tile designs, 56, pl.18; monogram design, 75

de Morgan, William, 40, 45, 86
Dodd, Francis, sketch of William Burton, pl.4
Doulton, 18
Dressler tunnel ovens, 14
Dunsany, Lord, 44
Duratino, Cipriano Piccolpasso, 41

English Ceramic Society, 11, 30
Evans, David, 64; figure, pl.118; bookends, pl.121
Evans, Joseph, 5
Evans, Josiah, 5
Evans, T. F., 20, 44, 66, pl.80; tile panel designs, 23
Exekias, 59, pl.54
Exhibitions, see Arts and Crafts, British Industries Fair, Brussels, Franco-British, Glasgow, Graves Gallery, Liège, Paris, Turin, Winnipeg

Firth family pottery, 43
Fisher, J., 44
Fletcher family, 5
Forsyth, Gordon, 44, 45, 87, pl.80; life, 59; Stoke School of Art, 47; influences, 59; books, 59; style, 45; identification marks, 75; bowl, pl.60; chargers, pl.64; figure group, pl.70; figure model, pl.72; goblet, pl.66; jug, pl.53; kylix, pl.55; mural designs, 22; plaque, pl.61; vases, pls.63, 65, 67-69

Fortuny, Escofet, 40
Franco-British Exhibition 1908, 21, 44, 64, pls.18, 39, 61, 116

George V, 44
Ginori, 40
Glasgow Exhibition 1901, 20, 53, 58, pls.36, 37
Glazes, 25ff; experiments by Joseph Burton, 11; development by Pilkington's, 25, 46; historical techniques, 25; eastern influences, 83, 84
Glazes, crystalline, 25, 83; aventurine, 26, 84; fiery crystalline, 84; sunstone, 26, 84; starry crystalline, 26, 84
Glazes, chicken and orange skin, 85; Cunian, 31, 46; eggshell/vellum, 26, 85; fruit skin, 85; golden lacquer, 85; lapis, 31, 46; metallic, 85; opalescents, 26, 85; starry-opalescent, 85; *sang-de-boeuf*, 43; transmutation, 30, 85; transparent tin oxide, 30
Graves' Gallery, 25, 40

Hall, Albert, 20, 66, pl.80; lustre tile, pl.35
Hall, Lawrence, 20, 66
Hanley Museum, 11
Heider, Maximilian von, 40
Howson-Taylor, W., 30, 40
Hughes, Fanny, 59

Identification marks, 75ff

Johnston, Edward, 11, 71
Jones, Jessie, 59; life, 64; vase, pl.116
Jones, T. B., 71
Joyce, Richard, 44, 46, 59, pl.97; life, 59; style, 45; identification marks, 75; pattern book, pls.43, 45; animal group, pl.74; bowls, pls.92, 94; lioness, pl.77; pig, pl.76; plaque, pl.91; vase design, pl.78; vases, pls.79, 81-90, 93, 95, 96

Kahler, Hermann A., 40
Kearsley Coal Co., 25
Kent, Edmund, 18, 20, 23, 65, pls.80, 100; designs, pl.34
Kilns, 12, 14, 41, 46
Kwiatowski, Joseph, 18, pl.1

Lancastrian Pottery, 15, 40, 25, 43-45; after 1951, 71; 1972-77, 15, 52, 76; identification marks, 75; retail outlets, 46; *Royal Lancastrian Pottery* (Lomax), 26, 31
Lapis ware, 31, 64, 88-89, pl.49
Lee-Wood, James, 10
Liberty, 46, pl.48
Liège International Exhibition, 43
Linton, W. S., 56
Lomax, Abraham, 25, 46; work on glazes, 25; paper on transparent tin-oxide glazes, 30; *Royal Lancastrian Pottery*, 26, 31
Lustreware, 86; history, 33-40; techniques, 40; Pilkington's methods, 41

*Magazine of Art*, 53
Manchester University, 11
Martin Brothers, 40
Massier, Clement, 40, 86
Maypole Dairies, 23, pl.13
McLoughlin, Mary, pl.98
Mendeleev, Dimitri, 25
Minton, Hollins & Co., 59
Moira, Gerald, 59
Moore, Bernard, 30, 40
Moore Bros., 60
Mucha, Alphonse, 20; *Les Fleurs*, pl.37
Murals, 22
Mycock, William S., 20, 44, 46, 59; pls.80, 98; life, 60; style, 45; identification marks, 75; bird studies, pl.46; bowls, pl.40, 111; designs, pl.40; plaques, pls.105, 112; Pueblo designs, pl.47; vases, pls.103, 104, 106-111

Northern Art Workers' guild, 58

Opus Sectile, 18

Paintresses, 19, 59, pl.11
Paris Exhibition 1900, 11, 22, 25, 40, 58, pl.22
Pilkington, Alfred, 10; Charles, 10; Dorothy, 50; Edward, 10; Laurence, 10; Margaret, 23, 50
Pilkington's company founded, 10; developments in 1890s, 12; in 1909, 18; during world wars, 12, 45; in 1930s, 46; in 1938, pl.2; finances, 12, 14, 50; changes of company name, 15; merger with Carter's, 15; royal warranty granted, 44

*Pottery Gazette*, 18
Prosser, Richard, 17

Radford, E. T., 43, 44, 47, 71, pl.31; identification marks, 75
Red Rose Guild of Handicrafts, 23
Rogers, Gladys M., 46, 59, pl.99; life, 60; decorations, pl.49; vases, pl.114
Roman tile manufacturer, 17
Rookwood Pottery, 84
Royal College of Science, Dublin, 11
Royal Lancastrian Pottery, *see* Lancastrian Pottery
Royal School of Mines, South Kensington, 10
Royal Society of Arts, 11
Rudd, J. H., 58
Ruskin Pottery, 30, 40

Seddon, J. P., 58
Sellars, J. M., 21
Sgraffito, 46, 64
Shields, Frederick, 20, 53
Simpson, Miss, 58; designs, pl.26
Society of Arts, 40
Spencer, John L., 47, 64; animal group, pl.74; model, pl.120; vase, pl.119
Stabler, Harold and Phoebe, 15
Steele, Florence, 58; designs, pls.25, 26
Storey, Annie, 59
*Studio*, 19, 58, 64, 66
*Studio Yearbook*, 66

Thomas, Harold, 47
Tiles, 17ff; history, 17; manufacture, 17-18; decoration methods, 17-18; cuenca, 18; Opus Sectile, 18; murals, 22
Titanic, 17, 65
Tooth, Henry, 60
Tunnicliffe, Robert, 43, 44; identification marks, 75
Turin International Exhibition 1911, 44
Turnbull & Stockdale, 53
Tyldsley, Ruth, 59

Vallance, Aylmer, 64
Voysey, C. F. A., 20; life, 58; designs, pl.19; *The Labours*, pls.20, 21

Walker Art Gallery murals, 22, pl.29
Wedgwood, Josiah, 83; on art, 48
Wedgwood & Sons, 10, 18, 19; lustreware, 40
Wedgwood Institute, Burton, 10
Wengers Ltd., 31
Winnipeg Industrial Exhibition 1898, 17
Wood, Edgar, 22

Yates, Annie, 59
Yates, John, pl.51

Zsolnay, 40